Colorado

OFF THE BEATEN PATH™

"Given the meticulous quality of Casewit's research, **Colorado: Off the Beaten Path** may well be the perfect guide for newcomers to our slice of the continent. . . . Offers a refreshing change of pace and a delightful new vision of our state."
    —KCFR Radio, Denver

"This book even holds surprises for natives or long-time inhabitants and will delight the mountain climber, the wildflower enthusiast . . . and the history buff."
    —*Colorado Outdoors*

"A fascinating guide that enables the reader to explore . . . little-known areas of the state. Using the book as an aid, you will discover your own Colorado."
    —*The News Tribune,* Fort Pierce/Port St. Lucie, Florida

"Anyone vacationing in Colorado will be well advised to take this slim paperback along."
    —*Sunday Cape Cod Times*

"Glows with its author's 40 years of Colorado experience."
    —*Piedmont Airlines*

D0939667

Colorado

OFF <u>THE</u> BEATEN PATH™

THIRD EDITION

CURTIS CASEWIT

A Voyager Book

The Globe Pequot Press

Old Saybrook, Connecticut

Cover map © DeLorme Mapping.

Art Credits: page 3, rendered courtesy of Denver Metro Convention & Visitors Bureau; page 39, based on a photograph by Carl Scofield; page 83, rendered courtesy of Larry Pierce/Steamboat Resort.

Library of Congress Cataloging-in-Publication Data
Casewit, Curtis W.
    Colorado: off the beaten path / by Curtis Casewit.—3rd ed.
        p.   cm.
    "A Voyager book."
    Includes index.
    ISBN 1-56440-399-8
    1. Colorado—Guidebooks.   I. Title.
F774.3.C37   1994
917.8804'33—dc20   94-11981
                                                              CIP

Manufactured in the United States of America
Third Edition/Second Printing

COLORADO

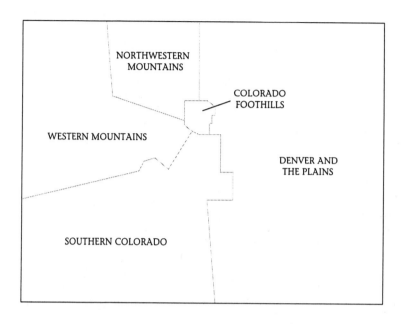

CONTENTS

INTRODUCTION

I first saw Colorado in 1948.

It was love at first sight. I have never been able to tear myself away, despite opportunities elsewhere. The state's beauty kept me here; indeed, there followed almost forty years of exploration. By automobile, train, plane. On foot and on horseback. On skis and on snowshoes.

From the tourist's viewpoint Colorado has everything one could desire; travelers spend around $6 billion here each year. The state even holds surprises for natives or longtime inhabitants. Indeed, after all those years of roaming through Colorado, I wrote this book in a constant state of amazement.

Denver itself is packed with the unexpected. And remarkably enough, you can drive a mere thirty minutes from the state capital to reach the swish and rush of mountain streams, view dramatic rocks, or wander among thick forests. Higher and higher mountains beckon to the west; to the east the placid plains offer new sights as well.

Colorado: Off the Beaten Path has assembled some of the state's most unique locales—some of which cannot be found in many travel books. The selections cover a wide area but are purely personal choices. Some of the attractions may be readily recognized but were visited and reviewed by this writer with a fresh slant. Many of the descriptions will be of interest to new settlers as well as those who have lived here for many decades. Naturally, suggestions for future editions are welcome.

ABOUT THE BOOK'S ORGANIZATION

Few people hereabouts know the names of counties. So each chapter deals with a *region*. In chapter 1, for instance, you visit the foothills and front range. Chapter 2 takes you along one of Colorado's main arteries—I–70—to famous western mountains, all the way from historic Georgetown to Glenwood Springs and beyond, with one or two side trips into nearby valleys. Where to next? It was logical to explore in chapter 3 the interesting sights of Colorado's northwestern mountains via the important US40 and the unusual Trail Ridge Road through the magnificent Rocky Mountain National Park. Chapter 4 deals with the state's southern region, including Colorado Springs. Lastly, Denver and the plains are the subjects of chapter 5. In every instance the focus was on the uniqueness of a destination.

Finally, a word about prices. Globe Pequot Press books aim to be practical, so the reader of *Colorado: Off the Beaten Path* deserves to know what to expect. The rates for hotels and restaurants are as follows: inexpensive, moderate, expensive. A few establishments get a "deluxe" label. Most of the state's hoteliers and restaurateurs believe in good values, though.

Happy traveling!

The prices and rates listed in this guidebook were confirmed at press time. We recommend, however, that you call establishments before traveling to obtain current information.

COLORADO FOOTHILLS

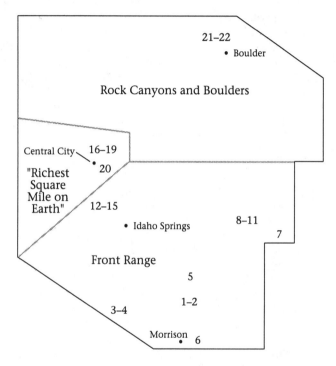

1. Red Rocks Park and Amphitheatre
2. Mount Falcon Park
3. Tiny Town
4. Glen-Isle on the Platte
5. Matthews-Winters Park
6. The Manor House
7. Healthy Habits
8. Geology Museum
9. Astor House Museum
10. Pioneer Museum
11. Railroad Museum
12. Buffalo Bill's Museum
13. Jefferson County Nature Center
14. Lookout Mountain
15. Beaver Brook Trail
16. St. Mary's Glacier
17. Central City Opera House
18. Eureka Street
19. Teller House Hotel
20. Black Forest Inn
21. Eldorado Springs Canyon
22. Boulder Canyon

COLORADO FOOTHILLS

FRONT RANGE

When you come upon the seventy-million-year-old ◆ **Red Rocks Park and Amphitheatre,** west of Denver, for the first time, the primeval scene takes your breath away: Huge reddish sandstone formations jut upward and outward. Each is higher than Niagara Falls. The view conjures up dinosaurs, sea serpents, and flying reptiles; indeed, tracks of those long-extinct creatures have been found here, along with valuable fossil fragments. The colors are those of the Grand Canyon; one can easily believe the geologists who speak of earth-shattering, monolith-building cataclysms, of retreating ancestral oceans, iron oxide color, water erosion. Geographers once called this site one of the Seven Wonders of the World.

The U.S. Geographical Survey showed up for eager surveys in 1868. By 1906 financier John Brisben Walker had acquired the land; the acoustics of these rocks would be perfect for an amphitheater. A visiting opera singer, Dame Nellie Melba, was quick to agree; it would make one of the world's greatest open-air stages. John Brisben Walker eventually donated the land to the community, and in 1927 it was incorporated into the Denver Mountain Parks System.

Construction started a few years later; dedication of the tiered outdoor area followed in 1941. The local symphony soon brought its famed orchestra to the site. The latter not only produced perfect sound and aesthetic inspiration but also allowed a magnificent look at Denver far below.

During many years the outdoor theater experienced triumphant ballet performances, and audiences heard celebrated orchestras and even portions of Wagner operas. Singers like Lily Pons, Jennie Tourel, and Helen Traubel all raved about the Red Rocks. Even the difficult-to-please Leopold Stokowski was impressed by a setting that included a "Creation Rock."

In 1959, in the interests of still further improvements, Denver's manager of parks flew to Germany at his own expense. He persuaded Wolfgang Wagner, grandson of the composer, to inspect Red Rocks. Wagner eventually remodeled the orchestra pit and made other design changes.

2

Red Rocks Amphitheatre

The cost of bringing large orchestras and opera companies proved to be financially difficult, however. What's more, performers sometimes fought with winds that would tear away the musician's notes or with sudden five-minute rains that would drench the singers to the depth of their costumes.

Since 1961 the Red Rocks rarely heard any more classical music; instead, by the mid-1960s the Beatles made a full-throttle appearance here. Through the seventies and eighties and into the nineties, there followed assorted high-decibel rock, pop, blues, jazz, and country western stars—often with sellouts of the 9,000 seats. Tickets are expensive. Fortunately, the public gets free admission at all other times. Traditionally, too, a free Easter Sunrise Service has taken place here for several decades. (The stage has meanwhile been covered.)

Red Rocks is easy to reach via numerous routes. From Denver you can take West Alameda Avenue west, drive US285 west, or follow I–70 west and watch for the marked exit. The total distance varies between 14 and 17 miles, depending on your route.

You can see the stunning Red Rocks Amphitheatre from the hiking trails of ◈ **Mount Falcon Park,** for which we can thank the same John Brisben Walker, financier, entrepreneur, visionary. Walker wanted to build a Summer White House in the park, and a marble plaque still indicates the spot. He had an eye for the best views: The Mount Falcon area is surrounded by blue mountains, and at a distance you can recognize Mt. Evans (elevation 14,264 feet) and the Continental Divide. Other vistas of the 1,415-acre Mount Falcon Park include the Colorado plains and, with a little imagination, Nebraska.

The park seems surprisingly serene; it is so vast that the walkers and horseback riders and mountain bikers can spread over many a flowered hill and dale. No motorcycles are permitted, and cars are restricted to a few parking lots—the latter concealed by trees. The exceptionally well-marked foot trails are often shaded by conifer forests. Picnic tables invite families, and there are meadows for kiters and butterfly fans. Lovers find privacy among the daisies, the scrub oak, and the spruce. Here, at 7,750 feet above sea level, a light breeze blows often. Summers are cooler here than in Denver, in the smog far below. For once, you hear only the light Colorado wind. The traffic has been silenced.

Walker's fortunes ultimately waned: The Summer White House was never built, and the financier's own castlelike home was struck by lightning in 1918 and burned. The stone walls and chimneys, and even the fireplaces, are still there—an interesting destination for hikers. A few minutes away, the stables do a good summer business. Cross-country skiers enjoy the park in winter.

Mount Falcon Park is accessible via Highway 8 to Morrison or via US285 and the Parmalee exit. Be prepared for dusty roads to the park entrance.

Surprise! Just twenty minutes west of Denver, the Big City—utter silence in a little-known park. To the north the famous Red

Rocks; to the south the little hamlet of Morrison, with its antiques stores.

The same US285 will take you to a truly offbeat family destination. Denverites, twenty minutes down the valley, know about ◈**Tiny Town;** out-of-town visitors probably haven't heard about this Lilliputian village and its miniature railway.

Tiny Town appeals to children. Imagine about one hundred toy-size, hand-crafted buildings! To peek into, sometimes to crawl into as well! Old mini–log cabins, fire station, post office, water tower, flourmill, bank, stables, schoolhouse, roominghouse, farms, ranches, barns and windmills, mines and miners' shacks, and many, many more. There's even a train ride around the entire Tiny Town village loop.

The attraction is run on a nonprofit basis by a foundation. The distance from Denver is about 12 miles via US285, turning south at South Turkey Creek Road. Bring a picnic and a couple of dollars for admission.

Open every day from Memorial Day Weekend through September, 10:00 A.M.–7:00 P.M. Open weekends in May and October, 10:00 A.M.–5:00 P.M. For more information: Tiny Town, 6249 South Turkey Creek Road, Morrison 80465; (303) 790–9393.

US285 is sometimes narrow and curvy, so it's easy to miss an entrance to an offbeat retreat for vacationers. One example? The modest little wooden sign that reads ◈**Glen-Isle on the Platte.** These humble log cabins and a well-worn lodge are hidden by a tiny bridge and assorted bushes and trees off the highway between Grant and Bailey. This unpretentious holiday settlement dates back to 1900 and works out fine for families, couples, and singles who want to cook (wood furnished) and who appreciate the silence of a 160-acre forest. The latter is honeycombed with footpaths for hikers; horse trails are nearby, too. Glen-Isle is nicely old-fashioned; the last time I visited, there was not even a television set. For folks who don't want to cook, a dining room offers homey food. The tab for everything seems reasonable enough. For more information: Glen-Isle on the Platte, Bailey 80421; (303) 838–5461.

◈**Matthews-Winters Park** derives its importance from location: The park lies astride the entrance to Mt. Vernon Canyon, which is one of the early routes to the gold fields of Central City (then known as the Gregory Diggings) and South

Park. Other canyons were also used, and at each portal a town was founded to try to get a share of the quick fortune the Fifty-niners were scrambling to uncover.

The park now consists of undulating grasslands, hiking trails (also used by horses), and fields of sedges, bleached in summer, silver-green sage, purple thistles, wild roses, and wild plums.

Sunflowers and chokecherries and willows lean over the gravestones and crosses of long-gone pioneers: I. R. DEAN, DIED AUGUST 12, 1860, AGED 31 YEARS, I AM AT REST. And the marker of a younger man: JAMES JUDY, DIED SEPTEMBER 8, 1867, AGED 21 YEARS.

Trails run through rabbit brush and tall dill, and there's nary a sound, despite the nearby highways.

The big year here was 1859. The stagecoaches and wagons rolled through, and the new town of Mt. Vernon had a 150-horse corral. A local paper declared that "timber, stone, lime and coal are abundant in the vicinity." For a while Mt. Vernon became a stage stop. An inn, a saloon, and a schoolhouse were built, used, abandoned. Once "boasting forty-four registered voters," the town of Mt. Vernon lost its place in history after the railroads arrived. And now? A few square gravestones, some crosses, and wild vegetation. Not far away, next to Mt. Vernon Creek, picnic tables sit under leafy trees.

The public parking area is located off SR26, just south of I–70, and lies within the platted Mt. Vernon town site. The park is open 5:00 A.M.–11:00 P.M.

The front range mountain settings come with precious few dinner retreats—particularly not historic ones like ◈ **The Manor House.** From afar the white Georgian mansion makes its appearance on top of a green hill, amid hiking trails and an equestrian center. White columns give the building a fairy-tale quality.

The Manor House was built on a vast ranch in 1914 by John C. Shaffer, industrialist, owner of the *Rocky Mountain News* (paper), importer of Hereford cattle from distant points, and collector of antiques. Shaffer's wife, Virginia, hosted President Theodore Roosevelt and other notable figures, who raved about the magnificent fireplaces, statuary, and elegant carpets and about the valuable nineteenth-century paintings. Various ranchers raised cattle nearby, with a view to faraway Denver. Virginia Shaffer wrote a poem about the landscape: "Where the sunsets are entrancing / where one sees a sight sublime / Come again! Come again!"

6

Now the elegant ranch house serves distinctive food in sumptuous surroundings. The restaurant is a little hard to get to: Look for US285 and exit at Highway C470, then to Ken-Caryl Avenue, to Mountain Laurel, and finally onto Manor House Road. It's a complicated trip, at least the first time. The thirty-minute drive from Denver is worthwhile, however. The Manor House has an imaginative chef who starts you off with wild mushroom strudel or smoked salmon (smoked right there), roast rack of lamb, veal medallions, and many more fine dishes, graced by elegant glassware and shining silver. Good service plus mountain views. The Manor House, 1 Manor House Road, Littleton 80127; (303) 973–8064.

If you travel west on US40 out of Denver, you abruptly leave behind the plains of Denver and eastern Colorado and enter a long valley with the jagged foothills of the Rockies rising on both sides. As you proceed, you may see some horses grazing on the slopes.

Hungry? There are not too many restaurants near the foothills. But as you drive west on West Colfax Avenue, make a stop at #14195 and get your healthy nourishment at ◆**Healthy Habits** restaurant (303–277–9293). It may be one of the secrets kept by diet-minded Denverites; here you get some sixty salads, buffet-style; an assortment of muffins; spinach and other pastas; and fresh fruit and other vegetarian fibers. Healthy Habits is a delightful place, especially in summer, when you can sit outdoors, "al fresco," and view the flower-dotted foothills from your table. It's a great break on your trip west to Golden.

Soon you reach the heart of Golden with its eight churches, all of them small and varied in architecture. The churches give the impression that even institutionalized religion can still be personal. Across the wide main street, just before you come to the bridge over Clear Creek, an arch shouts, HOWDY FOLKS, WELCOME TO GOLDEN, WHERE THE WEST REMAINS.

To the west there rise range after range of mountains, each higher than the next. These mountains, beside having whatever aesthetic or spiritual value you may find in them, serve the practical purpose of limiting the size to which Golden can grow—it currently has about 12,500 inhabitants. But the Rockies protected the city from becoming part of a growing urban sprawl.

The Golden story began back in 1859, when a man named Tom Golden set up a hunting camp with a couple of other men.

Soon some representatives of The Boston Company passed by on a wagon train, looking for a suitable place to establish a trading and supply base for the prospectors who were flooding the mining areas to the west. They liked the site and stayed.

Golden grew rapidly. Within a year it had a population of 700. By 1862 it became the territorial capital but lost this honor five years later to Denver. There was sporadic gold excitement in the immediate area—people still occasionally pan Clear Creak, west of town—but there were no big strikes. (The primary reward for panning here is the sight of gold in your pan. You can work all day for a dollar.) Its early economy was built on trading. It was the major supply center for the mining operations at Black Hawk, Central City, Idaho Springs, and other communities.

With the decline of mining, new economic bases emerged. Golden's present economy is based primarily on two institutions, both of which have brought it international recognition: the Colorado School of Mines, for a century the leading school in the world devoted to mining and minerals, and the Coors brewery, one of the largest in the country.

The Colorado School of Mines, while not open to the public for tours, does have a museum that fits in with the theme of the school. The ◆ **Geology Museum,** on the corner of Sixteenth and Maple on campus, is almost an art gallery. Murals by Irwin Hoffman depict many periods in the development and history of mining. See Egyptian slaves working a human-powered mill. Learn how Greeks and Romans mined by burning bushes over the area they wanted to excavate, then throwing cold water on the hot rocks, causing them to break apart. Open to the public; no fee is charged. Contact Colorado School of Mines, 1500 Illinois Street, Golden 80401; (303) 273–3000.

What does it mean, that slogan "Where the West remains," so proudly proclaimed on the banner? *West* is the most basic word in American folklore. Its connotations extend well into the realms of history, morality, and philosophy. To the tourist, out to see the country, it's obviously a matter of history. What could possibly be more "west" than the place where Buffalo Bill asked to be buried? If that's not enough, the traveler can visit the ◆ **Astor House Museum** and the ◆ **Pioneer Museum.**

The Colorado ◆ **Railroad Museum** displays many ancient, narrow-gauge locomotives and even a depot. The narrow-gauge

railroads of Colorado made it possible for miners and other for-
tune seekers to access the mineral riches of the Rocky Mountains.
These tracks also allowed the wealth to be carried out and spread.
The history of railroads in Colorado is preserved in the twelve-acre
Colorado Railroad Museum.

Here you will see the original "rolling stock," including locomotives. A rail spur allows the facility to "steam up" different
engines through the year.

The building itself, a masonry replica of an 1880 depot, houses
some 50,000 photographs and artifacts. The basement contains
one of the state's largest model railroad exhibits. It re-creates some
of Colorado's old rail lines, such as the one in Cripple Creek.
Famous relics of the museum include the Rio Grande Southern
1931 "Galloping Goose No. 2" and the steel observation car used
on the Santa Fe Super Chief, the "Navajo." A bookstore sells about
1,000 titles and magazines, tapes, gifts, and mementos.

Open every day except Christmas and Thanksgiving. Hours are
9:00 A.M. to 5:00 P.M., September–May; 9:00 A.M. to 6:00 P.M.,
June–August. Admission is $3.00 for adults and $1.50 for children. Colorado Railroad Museum, 17155 West Forty-fourth
Avenue, Golden 80401; (800) 365–6263 or (303) 279–4591.

If the West remains here in Golden in any living sense, it can
only be in the character of the people.

What kind of people were they? As with any pioneers, they had
to be extremely self-reliant. They were dissatisfied with what they
had left behind and were willing to take all necessary risks to try to
find something better. They were doers rather than theoreticians.

The Golden folks love the outdoors. Everywhere there are
campers, tents, jeeps. Backpackers can be seen heading out of
town toward the mountains. The cultural life seems aimed at
"doing" rather than the less demanding "appreciating." For
example, the Foothills Art Center devotes its major effort to
workshops and lessons along with the display of art.

For all this, and much more, Golden is certainly worth a visit.
Additional information: Chamber of Commerce, 611 Fourteenth
Street, Golden 80402; (303) 279–3113.

Buffalo Bill was a unique character of the frontier. And the
museum that bears his name, 12 miles west of central Denver, on
Lookout Mountain, has a unique western character. Here are the
mementos that bring a fascinating man to life: the paintings and

posters that show him in full regalia on his white horse, white of beard, cowboy hat jaunty on his head. You can see his clothes, saddles, old weapons, even a mounted buffalo, and lots of artifacts. (In 1989 Buffalo Bill's museum and grave attracted 53,000 visitors.)

❖ **Buffalo Bill's Museum** is crammed with photographs that retrace his careers as a buffalo hunter, Indian fighter, army scout (for U.S. Army General Sheridan, among others).

Born as William F. Cody, Buffalo Bill led an extraordinary life. As a longtime Pony Express rider, he was pursued by Indians, escaping (as he wrote), "by laying flat on the back of my fast steed. I made a 24-mile straight run on one horse." On another occasion he rode 320 miles in some twenty-one hours to deliver the mails. (En route he exhausted twenty horses for the journey.) He had few rivals as a hunter and was said to have shot 4,280 bison in a 1½-year period. His slogan: "Never missed and never will / always aims and shoots to kill."

The buffalo shooting had a purpose, of course; the meat was needed to feed some 1,200 men who were laying track for the railroad. And though William Cody had his battles with the Indians, he later learned the Sioux language and befriended the Cheyennes, among other tribes.

William Cody may have had his best times as a circus rider, actor, and showman, gaining fame all over the world. The first "Buffalo Bill's Wild West" show opened in 1883. The extravaganza toured for nearly three decades, spreading the myths and legends of the American West around the globe. Almost a hundred mounted Sioux Indians chased wagon trains and a stagecoach; Annie Oakley and Johnny Baker amazed audiences with their marksmanship; eighty-three cowboys rode bucking broncos, thereby formalizing a cowboy sport into rodeo; and the entire Battle of Little Big Horn was re-created. Spectators could see live elk and deer from Colorado. There were horse races and even a bison hunt complete with a charging herd. At its height Buffalo Bill's show employed more than 600 performers. And in one year he traveled 10,000 miles, performing in 132 cities in 190 days.

Cody's flowing white hair, his short white beard and rifle-holding figure symbolized the Wild West in many European capitals. Buffalo Bill gave a command performance for Queen Victoria at Windsor Castle and amused Kaiser Wilhelm II in Berlin.

No fewer than 557 dime novels were written about Cody during his lifetime. His face beamed out from hundreds of thousands of posters. Even today the distinctive goatee and silver hair continue to make him more recognizable than the kings, generals, and presidents who may have honored him.

Cody made one of the first movie Westerns ever produced. Although near the end of his career, he also lived to see the start of the tourist industry as he opened the first hotel near Yellowstone National Park.

Toward the end of his life, he turned into an entrepreneur and author. He gave most of his life's savings away to various good causes.

His money ran out; his fame did not.

When Buffalo Bill died, President Woodrow Wilson wired his condolences. Former president Teddy Roosevelt called Cody "an American of Americans." The Colorado legislature passed a special resolution ordering that his body lie in state under the gold-plated rotunda of the State Capitol in Denver. Nearly 25,000 people turned out to pay their last respects and march in his funeral on Memorial Day, June 3, 1917.

Buffalo Bill's grave is a few steps from the museum atop Lookout Mountain, with a good view of Denver and the plains. Anyone can come and see the burial place. It is marked by white pebbles. The simple legend reads: WILLIAM F. CODY 1846–1917.

The museum stands in a quiet conifer forest. First opened in 1919, it has been restored and improved over the years. A gift shop sells arrowheads, carpets, and other fitting items.

The hours are 9:00 A.M.–4:00 P.M. daily in winter, except Mondays; 9:00 A.M.–5:00 P.M. daily in summer. Call (303) 526–0747. Small fee. For the most scenic drive, take US6 west of Denver to Golden, turn left on Nineteenth Street, and proceed uphill via Lookout Mountain Road, also called Lariat Trail because it twists and turns all the way up Lookout Mountain.

As you continue south on Lookout Mountain Road after leaving Buffalo Bill's grave, a sign on Colorow Road will direct you to turn right toward the ◆Jefferson County Nature Center. Situated on 110 acres of a fenced nature preserve, the center has a museum, plant and animal displays, and a self-guiding nature trail. All are handicapped-accessible, and admission is free. Hours are 10:00 A.M. to 4:00 P.M. Tuesday through Sunday; the facility is

11

closed Mondays and holidays. Also offered are nature classes that range from "The Secret Language of Snow" to wildflower and bird walks to night tours to discover constellations and nocturnal animal activity. All sessions require preregistration. Contact the nature center at 910 Colorow Road, Golden 80401; (303) 526–0594.

Never mind, all you rock climbers! Step aside, you hardy mountaineers! Make room for some hiking tourists—the sort who can spare only a couple of hours or so for a gentle excursion into the Colorado front range. Easy, mountain flower-bordered trails abound in the foothills near the state capital.

One of the least-known paths curves around ◆**Lookout Mountain,** which was first used by the Cheyenne and Arapaho Indians as a lookout. Now known as the ◆**Beaver Brook Trail,** it is one of the state's most interesting paths, yielding views of the gorges below, dipping and climbing with a varied landscape of leaf trees and dramatic Douglas fir. Although you're close to Denver, you're quickly led away from civilization.

Instead of highways there are fields of asters, yucca, and wild roses under you. In the forests the path is moss bordered, and spring beauties show their heads in season.

The Beaver Brook Trail makes some demands on your balance because you need to maneuver across several small boulder fields, which really amounts to an easy level of rock climbing. Going on for about 7 miles, Beaver Brook remains blissfully quiet during the week. On Sundays, however, you sometimes see church groups and long lines of scouts and other hikers coming up from the city. If you hike up here in July and August, you'll be surrounded by lots of color. On the trail you may also spot the state flower, the blue Rocky Mountain columbine.

It's true that wildflowers bloom later at the higher elevations. By the time plants have already wilted above Golden (elevation 7,600 feet), other flowers on the Beaver Brook Trail just begin to unfold. The higher you climb, the later the growth, the smaller the flower, and the colder the air.

Small Colorado plants appear and disappear with the seasons, go underground, or take many years to mature. Wonders? Certain wildflowers can sleep peacefully under the thickest snow cover, biding their time until spring. In summer the large fields of mountain flowers on the Beaver Brook Trail meadows give pleasure to your eyes.

The Beaver Brook Trail is within easy reach from Denver by car. Just take US6, turn left at the first traffic light (Nineteenth Street) in Golden, then drive up the curvy SR68 for 3 miles. Before you get to Buffalo Bill's grave, you spot a sign on your right: BEAVER BROOK TRAIL: WINDY SADDLE ENTRANCE.

They always called it a glacier. But this Colorado remnant of the Ice Age is actually an icefield, covering a steep year-round snowbowl of about ten acres. In summer, when Denver swelters in an 95° heat wave, it's about 45° on the glacier, and young people come to ski here in July and August. Other visitors to the famous snowfield bring platters or auto tubes or even race downhill on shovels. Hikers, campers, and backpackers can be seen at the 11,000-foot level as they scramble uphill past the last scrub pines. A few tourists come to sit on rocks and soak up the Colorado sun.

All that eternal snow and ice make ◆ **St. Mary's Glacier** unusual, of course. The trip is a pleasant one, attracting Sunday drivers from the Big City. Once you exit I–70, you follow a creek, flanked by stands of conifers and aspen trees. After about 8 miles the road steepens and leads into a series of driver-challenging curves and serpentines. Then the valley widens and the forest thickens. You see several rushing waterfalls. At elevation 10,400 feet you notice a free parking lot; leave your car and hike up the rocky jeep trail or follow the uphill footpaths through kinnikinnik, past the many fallen trees that age gracefully in gray. On weekends you meet lots of families on your way up to the glacier. People are friendly and talkative. "Been to the top yet? How was it? Do we have far to go?"

After half an hour you see a cold lake, topped by the glacier. It's less harmless than most folks think. Mountain dwellers know St. Mary's record: Each year someone who skis too fast or careens downhill on a shovel somehow gets bruised, bloodied, or even killed. On occasion cross-country skiers are buried by an avalanche up here. In winter the ill-prepared, ill-clothed can get frostbitten on top of the glacier, at the 11,400-foot level. The prudent know that mountains are unforgiving; these visitors come to St. Mary's only when it smiles.

Follow I–70 just past Idaho Springs; then take exit 238, known as the Fall River Road. A 12-mile drive brings you to the parking lot and the start of your St. Mary's Glacier adventure.

13

Richest Square Mile on Earth

The ◆ **Central City Opera House** seldom misses an opportunity to stage operas having to do with Colorado's past. During one season, for instance, the *Ballad of Baby Doe* proved to be a most appropriate work. The Baby Doe Tabor story deals with the lavish Colorado mining riches more than one hundred years ago.

At one point in history, Central City vied with Leadville for the bonanzas. They called Central City the Richest Square Mile on Earth. In all, some $75 million in gold was found there. Tourists can still do a bit of gold panning in nearby creeks. And through Labor Day you can ride a re-created narrow-gauge railway along the bleached mountain sides, past the old abandoned mounds of earth, mines of yesteryear.

Sloping, winding ◆ **Eureka Street** has been kept up. The red brick buildings look as well preserved as those of Denver's restored Larimer Square. Central City's pharmacy and several other stores put their oldest relics into the windows. The ancient ◆ **Teller House Hotel** is crammed with magnificent old clocks, armoires, rolltop desks, velvet sofas, and antique phones. A rediscovery of Victorian times, still worth visiting today. (Such plushness came with an original price tag of $107,000 for the hotel.)

The Teller House and the well-appointed old Opera House contrast with the miners' dwellings. They're small, modest cubes scattered across the pale gold or ochre and russet slopes.

The first frame houses sprang up during the 1860s, along with the mine dumps. Gold! Not just in a river but in the mountain, too. A man named John Gregory had plodded to 8,500-foot-high Central City from Denver, a trip of some 35 miles with an elevation gain of more than 3,000 feet.

That was in 1859. Gregory soon dug up a fortune. The word raced as fast as the spring waters of Clear Creek. Horace Greeley, the New York editor, heard about Gregory Gulch and traveled west to take a personal look. Greeley reported: "As yet the entire population of the valley, which cannot number less than four thousand, sleep in tents or under pine boughs, cooking and eating in the open air."

A mass of prospectors swarmed into the hillsides. Some people had a grand time. A theater was built. Sarah Bernhardt and Edwin Booth came to perform. The Teller House Hotel rose in 1872,

14

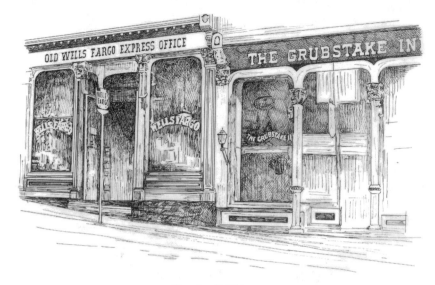

Central City

attracting the finest artisans. Large, carved bedsteads, marble-topped commodes, tall rosewood and walnut highboys were ferried across the prairies and up the rough roads by ox team and mule and on wood-burning trains. Central City's hotel hosted famous people. President Ulysses S. Grant, Walt Whitman, Oscar Wilde, Baron de Rothschild, and assorted European noblemen and their wives all slept in Central City.

In 1874 most of the community burned down. But gold rebuilt it. Less than four years later, there was a new opera house, which still stands. Through the decades the small, warm, intimate 756-seat theater fetched major productions, including opera staples like *Tosca, Manon, The Merry Widow, Rigoletto,* and *La Traviata*. All the operas are sung in English, in addition to the British D'Oyly Carte Company's *Yeoman of the Guard*.

Opening night remains Colorado's great social event. The cars climb the road along Clear Creek Canyon, the same route taken by John Gregory more than one hundred years ago.

Now masses of gamblers also swarm into the area, since gaming was approved for Central City and Black Hawk. New casinos have replaced many historic buildings and shops. Where parking was once hard to find, it is now almost impossible, but shuttle services run from Golden and other areas in Denver on a regular basis.

If you want to try your luck, stop at these Central City establishments: Dostal Alley, Silver Slipper, Doc Holiday Ltd., Long Branch Saloon, Annie Oakley's, Glory Hole, and Bullwhackers.

Down the road in Black Hawk, try Otto's at the Black Forest Inn, Crook's Palace, and Lilly Belle's.

Central City is about an hour's drive from Denver via US6. Performances take place in the Victorian Opera House, on Eureka Street, in June and July. For exact dates and productions, call (303) 292–6700, or write 621 Seventeenth Street, Denver 80293.

The ◆ **Black Forest Inn** at Black Hawk is worth the fifteen-minute detour from Idaho Springs through the picturesque Clear Creek Canyon. The restaurant is the lair of owner Bill Lorenz, a German who built a reputation for schnitzel, sauerbraten, goulash, pork loins, wild game, and other specialties a la Deutsch. Try the oxtail soup for an appetizer and order German wines or beers. The restaurant's Gregory Hall accommodates groups of 200.

Herr Lorenz is always on hand, supervising his staff among the expected trappings of cuckoo clocks, tapestries that depict old Rhine castles, and antlered trophies. The Black Forest is open all year, except for January weekdays, when Herr Lorenz often goes home to Germany. His inn offers meals only—no accommodations.

Hours are daily 11:00 A.M.–9:30 P.M.; Sundays 11:00 A.M.–8:00 P.M.; closed Mondays except in summer. Meals here are expensive but worth it. You reach the inn via US6 and Colorado Highway 119; turn left at Black Hawk. Phone: (303) 279–2333.

ROCK CANYONS AND BOULDERS

It is still early when the jeep pulls into ◆ **Eldorado Springs Canyon,** swishes across an oiled road, and comes to a stop. There are four in the vehicle: three physicians and a broad-shouldered mountain climber who has roamed 20,000-foot altitudes. For a weekend even 2,000 feet of climbing will do. As long as there is a technical challenge.

The challenge could be one of the Flatiron rocks, especially the Third. The names carry messages: Naked Edge is one of the state's hardest climbing routes; Red Garden Wall is sheer verticality.

16

Already, from the road, the climbers can see the dark brown slab slicing the lightening sky, daring the men. They shoulder their lead-heavy packs and wind their way to the base of the cliff. Here they unpack their gear: nylon ropes, neatly coiled; dozens of chocks—steel spikes—of all sizes and colors; water and food for an exhausting day.

At 8:00 A.M. the stone face still remains in the shadows. It shoots up straight. Few handholds or footholds.

The men peer up, craning their necks at the opponent. Now they fasten the hardware around their midriffs and form two parties who will attack the rock face at separate points. Here they rope in silently, purposefully. One man begins to scale his way up from the road 100 yards to his left; then another lead starts up. In each party only one person at a time does the climbing. Very, very slowly.

When the sun finally hits the granite and the tourists arrive, the Boulder men have gained only 70 feet. For the bystander there is not much drama here. Only precision and caution and labor. By early afternoon the four challengers have made the top. A total gain of 800 vertical feet. The Coloradans feel a great sense of achievement.

Vertical adventures are to be found all over this state, the climbing and mountaineering magnet of Mainland U.S.A. Colorado's average altitude is a lofty 6,800 feet; this state contains more than 75 percent of all the land above 10,000 feet in the United States. The Boulder area is especially popular.

For the good rock climber, Eldorado Springs Canyon provides many of the region's hardest challenges. Today the magnificently sheer walls attract close to 50,000 climbing attempts each year. Hundreds of possible routes exist on the canyon's many major cliffs.

Every top climber has a personal list of the most difficult ascents in the Boulder mountain area and lots of stories as well. Some of the most notorious feats are Psycho, Jules Verne, Vertigo, and the Diving Board, all in Eldorado Springs or vicinity.

◆ **Boulder Canyon** and the Flatirons area feature such eloquently named hair-raisers as Death and Transfiguration, Country Club Crack, and Tongo.

The Third Flatiron is one of the most famous destinations, attracting many Boulder collegians. Most require two to five

17

hours to reach the 1,400-foot crest, which happens to be even higher than New York's Empire State Building. Colorado's leading rock specialists are able to do the job in half an hour. The record is twelve minutes.

Spectators can watch the performances from below.

In essence the sport is an elegant form of gymnastics. Strength, form, and rhythm become more important than endurance. Years back the object was to reach a wall or peak via the safest and most convenient route. After the turn of the century, small groups of Colorado mountaineers began to evolve the modern-day philosophy. Rock climbing now became an art form—a delicate vertical ballet choreographed by the peculiarities of the rock itself. (Most climbers wear ballet-type light, flexible climbing shoes; others "dance" on the rock in their bare feet.)

A Colorado wall can involve the mind like a chess game. The expert studies his target from level ground and then keeps studying the route all along the way up. Bill Forrest, a well-known Denver-based expert who sometimes shows up in Eldorado Canyon, underlines this subtle interplay of mind and body. "A major part of climbing is *looking,*" Forrest says. "Look with the fingers and feet as well as with the eyes. A leader must employ all senses to scrutinize a wall and to seek protection possibilities."

Top leaders choose each foot- and handhold with care. They test rock. Will it hold? Could it crumble? Is that crack too high up to be reached? Even on easier pitches experienced climbers make it a habit to pick their steps with deliberation. No hasty moves. No slipping. No falling. Besides, the climber must have three points of contact with the rock. The contact can be two hands and one foot, or one hand and two feet. (Knees are never used.) Nor do skilled climbers grip bushes, small trees, or other vegetable holds. Plants seldom grow deep roots in rocky country.

A proper position also separates the novice from the expert. New climbers often lean *into* the mountain, hugging it. Experts know that it is better to keep the upper body *away* from the rock. So they lean out and look up. They develop rhythm. This way they surmount every hurdle.

How do you get started? Boulder's Colorado Mountain Club chapter organizes a yearly school for all comers. The Mountain Rescue Group has taught mountaineering, and the elders of the American Alpine Club and the local Sierra Club chapter take up their members for lessons. Mountaineering schools or individual instructors are often connected with Boulder climbing-equipment shops, where you can find out details. And lastly, the University of Colorado organizes some special summer programs for first-timers. As a result of all these and other possibilities, Boulder has more rock enthusiasts per capita than any other city of 91,000 inhabitants.

Actually, rock climbing isn't too difficult to learn. Any moderately athletic person can pick up basic techniques in a couple of days. ("It's the soul that counts, not the body," says one guide.) Being in condition helps.

On the Colorado cliffs the two major maneuvers are (1) the *belay,* a stance allowing you to protect your teammates by means of a rope, and (2) the *rappel,* which helps you to get down any steep wall. Only the first step over the void takes courage; the rest of the downward journey is easy, in the company of experienced guides.

Some authorities consider bouldering the best practice. Bouldering is a means of training; it allows you to scale difficult rock sections close to the ground. Even experts can be seen on Eldorado Canyon boulders testing themselves against strenuous/hairy sequences of 6 to 8 feet off the ground. This practice prepares them for similar terrain higher up.

Generally, most local routes offer quick escapes if the weather turns bad. An exception: the east face of the Third Flatiron. This panoramic climb is generally underestimated by novices. Sudden meteorological changes can be the undoing here. Other beginners may underestimate the difficulty of an ascent and overestimate their skills. Likewise, guides warn tyros that they must never venture into the high terrain on their own. The Boulder-based Rocky Mountain Rescue Group performs an average of 120 rescue operations each year in the area. Many such missions are the result of the inexperienced getting into trouble, sometimes resulting in injuries—broken ankles, legs, backs, or head traumas—or even death.

Good climbers respect these mountains and at the same time savor the aesthetics. They see the beauty of the scenery. To be sure, Eldorado Canyon seems different from one day to the next. You observe subtle light changes. The stone may now be dark blue, now orange, now golden. It can look harsh or delicate. A sudden prism of light can illuminate a meadow below and sharpen the crests above. So each trip is new. You will climb peaks in delightfully soft sunshine or under ultraviolet rays that tan even the palest faces. You drink, and water never tasted so sweet. Food—any food—goes down remarkably well after the day's clambering across Colorado's rocks.

Fortunately, you're never by yourself. Solo climbing is insanity and reserved for a few rare hermits. For the average person lone rockmanship remains nearly impossible. The climbing ropes require several people. Safety comes in numbers of two or more. The popularity of the sport, however, means that desirable areas like Eldorado Canyon can be quite crowded at times.

On a rope personal values change. Speaking the truth, helping, adapting, persevering become important. Human contacts come faster. When at its best, mountaineering can bring human beings closer together. Woodrow Wilson Sayre, a climber and professor of philosophy, once put it this way: "Real friendship is increasingly difficult to maintain. We hurry so much, we move, we change jobs, we juggle a hundred responsibilities. How often do we see our best friend? If we hardly see them, can we really share joy and tragedy with them? I think we crave a deeper sort of friendship. If we don't have it, we miss something very important in life. Friends are made for the close warmth tested in the mountains."

Eldorado Springs is about 25 miles northwest of Denver via the Boulder Turnpike, SR128, SR93, and SR170; the area is 7 miles south of Boulder via SR93 and SR170.

WESTERN MOUNTAINS

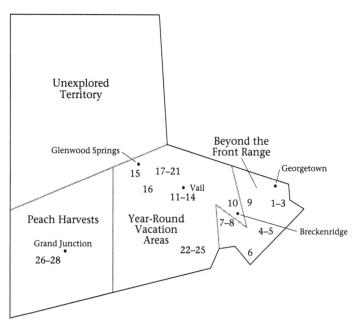

Unexplored
Territory

Glenwood Springs

Beyond the
Front Range

Georgetown

15   17–21

16   • Vail
11–14

10 9   1–3

7–8

Peach Harvests

Year-Round
Vacation
Areas

Grand Junction

22–25

4–5   Breckenridge

6

26–28

1. Georgetown
2. Georgetown Loop Railroad
3. Hotel de Paris
4. Mt. Evans
5. Echo Lake
6. Tumbling River Ranch
7. Lake Dillon
8. Ski-and-Yachting Regatta
9. Eisenhower Tunnel
10. Breckenridge
11. Colorado Ski Museum
12. Vail Public Library
13. Gore Range
14. The Betty Ford Alpine
    Gardens
15. Glenwood Hot Springs

16. White River National Forest
17. Hanging Lake
18. Strawberry Days
19. Fall Art Festival
20. Hot Springs Lodge
21. Kaiser House
22. Hotel Colorado
23. Redstone Inn
24. Cleveholm Manor
25. Hotel Jerome
26. Clark Family Peach Orchards
27. Cross Orchards Living History
    Farm
28. Colorado National
    Monument

Western Mountains

Beyond the Front Range

"The forests are shouting with color," John Steinbeck once wrote.

It's the sudden September frost that produces the spectacle that exalts Coloradans, brings them out of their homes and offices, autumn after autumn. Look into the local newspapers; follow the color photographers, the Sunday painters, the young couples. Exodus to the Rockies! See the aspen trees! The leaves suddenly turn on like so many bright lights. They dazzle. They glow among the deep green of the firs. There are entire aspen forests in these mountains.

The largest groves generally are found between elevations of 8,000 to 10,000 feet. Colors start at the higher elevations and spread their way down as the season progresses. A bright golden yellow predominates, with varying shades of brilliant reds, browns, and oranges interspersed with the green of the slower changing leaves and the surrounding conifers.

There is a lyrical something about these "quaking" trees when you're alone among them; the golden leaves tremble in the slight breeze, make a gentle sound of applause, talk to themselves, or send messages to the raspberry bushes. You'll see the gold and copper all over the state from the end of September through early October. In Aspen itself, in Winter Park, along the Rampart Range Road from Colorado Springs to Sedalia, beside the Peak-to-Peak Highway between Nederland and Allenspark, west of Boulder. "Aren't the aspen beautiful?" people ask, setting out to see them before winter blows down from the Rockies. Of course, it depends on how much time you have. Six hours? A day? Two? Then consider a good circle tour: Denver, Idaho Springs, Silver Plume, Breckenridge, Fairplay, Denver. No toll roads. Easy motoring.

Begin with US6, the more spectacular because it's carved out of deep canyons, where the upper rocks are highlighted by the sun. Up to the little mountain community of Idaho Springs (altitude 7,540 feet), on I–70, with the peaks rising on both sides. The aspen trees shine like so many lamps among the fir and spruce, and after you're through Georgetown (which is worth visiting), you seem to be in the Alps: The mountains go up steeply now, and the valley's narrow. Up, up to the Continental Divide (11,992 feet) and down from the massive Loveland Pass to the Dillon reservoir. The sun skips across these lake waters with their small marina sailboats, fishing boats, canoes! In Frisco swing left onto SR9, which still circles this handsome reservoir. Grasslands now, gold, brown, green, leading to the pivot of the tour. Breckenridge!

This little mining community is once more on the verge of a bonanza. In 1859 it was gold. Now it's real estate and second homes for airline people, retired corporation presidents, and skiers. Yet you couldn't tell this boom from the looks and feeling here. Breckenridge remains congenial, unpretentious, informal, western. The children are running across the silent brown pine needles; some teenagers fish for trout in the transparent Blue River.

One of the local cowboys packs families into the backcountry for a horseback ride or for hunting deer, and another entrepreneur sends jeeps into the wilderness. (The driver acts as a guide.) At the west part of town, though, there is civilization in the shape of too many condominiums.

It's peaceful again as you drive through thick forests past beaver ponds to little-known, ever-so-gentle Hoosier Pass. Golden brown-yellow meadows, faded green lichened rocks—and hardly a house in sight. Impressive 14,000-foot peaks all around: Quandary Peak, Mt. Lincoln, Mt. Sherman. Placer Valley, where the aspen trees brighten the pine woods. With a population of 500, Fairplay is the "big" town now, but you're through quickly. Suddenly, clouds in this bright-blue sky; a quick autumn rain. The horses and cows and sheep stand in these darkening fields patiently while the water comes down. Half an hour later, along the South Platte River, the sun bursts through the trees again. At Grant US285 narrows and curves along the river past nice campsites that should be full but aren't. (Few tourists after Labor Day.) All the way to Denver, the names spell nature, forest, Colorado.

Pine Junction. Deer Creek. Conifer. Indian Hills. Aspen Park.

A few last golden aspen trees followed by russets and reds of maples and oaks. Then Morrison, where the orchards are thick with purple apples. At the lower altitude, and out of the mountains, the air warms you once more. Pleasant autumn. After some 175 miles the Colorado circle tour ends where it began. But what a six-hour world between!

From US6, west of Denver, follow I–70 to Frisco, then SR9 through Breckenridge to Fairplay, from where you return to Denver via US285.

In autumn the wind whistles through the well-kept streets of ◆ **Georgetown,** rattling the windows of the impeccable Victorian houses. The winter snows pile up high here, and spring is slow to come at an elevation 8,500 feet above sea level. The mountains rise so steeply on all four sides of Georgetown that even the summers are cool; the sun shines for only a few hours.

Yet this community 45 miles west of Denver has more ambience, more sightseeing, more genuine concern for its own history than most other Colorado cities. It is special in its own way. The city fathers have spent six-figure sums to rebuild and preserve the pink brick houses, the old-time saloons, the museums that conjure up the last century of gold and silver riches. The antiques shops, silversmiths, and weavers are among the best in the state. The craft shops are different, real, worth browsing in, and much better than those of Vail or other fancy ski resorts to the west.

Unlike Vail, which rose from a cow pasture, Georgetown is a historic community. And proud of it.

On a clear spring day in 1859, two prospecting brothers, George and David Griffith, struggled their way up Clear Creek searching for minerals. Unsuccessful at the other mining camps in Colorado, they reached out for new untried land, and this time they had luck—they found gold.

After the discovery the Griffith brothers did a highly unusual thing for prospectors—instead of just digging up the mountain and leaving with their wealth, they brought their entire family out from Kentucky to live permanently in their valley. The tiny settlement they founded became known as George's Town, and although no more significant strikes were made, it grew steadily for five years.

Then, in 1884, assays showed an extremely high silver content. The boom was on. Over the next thirty years, the mines in and around Georgetown produced more than $200 million worth of silver. The town became known as the Silver Queen of the Mountains—and in 1868 it was named Georgetown.

By 1880 some 10,000 people made the city their home. The building of fortunes, houses, and reputations flourished. Elaborate mansions attested to wealth. Hotels served the finest cuisine in gilt rooms with elegant furniture. An Opera House brought Broadway productions and favorite classical operas to the wealthy.

All this came to an abrupt end; the silver panic of 1893 hit hard, with silver prices dropping to almost nothing. Mines, mills, and livelihoods vanished. The town became the ghost of its past glory.

Georgetown rested for more than six decades. Then tourism came, and interstate highways transported millions of tourists to the high mountains.

And a historical transportation mode was reconstructed to bring these tourists to Georgetown. The ◆ **Georgetown Loop Railroad** was originally completed in 1877. The goal of the railroad company was to reach another mining boom town—Leadville.

They never made it.

Instead, the workers pushed on just another 2 miles to Silver Plume, a mining camp up the valley. Even this short distance created difficult engineering problems.

Just 2 miles away, Silver Plume was 600 feet higher in elevation. To complete the spur to the next mountain stop, the rail tracks had to cover 4½ miles.

As the automobile gained popularity and the mining industry collapsed, the Loop was abandoned. The bridge and rails were used as scrap metal. The spur was forgotten and overgrown with weeds for thirty-five years.

Then the Colorado Historical Society stepped in, bought the land, and set about the major task of rebuilding the tracks and the bridge. In 1984, the new Devil's Gate bridge was opened.

The Georgetown Loop has been running ever since.

An eighty-minute ride takes you from historic Georgetown to Silver Plume and back, crossing the Devil's Gate trestle bridge. Views from the open cars are panoramic. Bighorn sheep may be seen in addition to other valley wildlife. In autumn the aspens offer a gilded view of this same mountain scenery. Phone (303) 569–2403 for times and prices.

Unlike other Colorado mining towns, Georgetown was never totally destroyed by fire, so today it has more than 200 carefully preserved historic buildings.

Luckily, too, Georgetown passed a historic preservation ordinance many years ago. The local historical society is serious about its purpose. One of Georgetown's landmarks is the French-style ◆ **Hotel de Paris,** now a museum full of Tiffany fixtures, lace curtains, and hand-carved furniture. (Open May to September, 9:00 A.M.–5:00 P.M. Small charge. Phone 303–569–2311.) Georgetown has several Victorian mansions worth seeing. During the first two December weekends, a well-known Christmas market with small booths and outdoor stalls beckons. One of the best inquiry points: Polly Chandler, in Polly's Book Store, 505 Rose Street; (303) 569–3303. She really knows the town.

For more information write the Chamber of Commerce, P.O. Box 667, Georgetown 80444-0667; (303) 569–2888. From Denver Georgetown can be reached via I–70 west in about an hour.

"It was awesome," former Miami resident Steve Cohen told friends in Florida. "We looked down at the passing clouds. You felt as though you'd reached the top of the world."

The traveler was referring to the highest paved auto road in the United States, leading from Idaho Springs, west of Denver, to the top of 14,264-foot-high ◆ **Mt. Evans.** The mountain first attracted gold-hungry prospectors during the nineteenth century; it was named in 1870 after Governor John Evans. A few years earlier famous artist Albert Bierstadt and a friend had climbed it. Bierstadt's paintings express the grandeur of this and other high Colorado peaks.

Pick a sunny summer day to make your drive up to the summit. Unlike on Pikes Peak, near Colorado Springs, you need pay no toll to reach the top of Mt. Evans. Keep in mind that the road above the 10,600-foot level is open only from late June through Labor Day; if you want to conquer the peak in winter, you'll have to do so on snowshoes or cross-country skis.

What are the attractions of this summer drive? For one thing, you get to see a lot of scenery. The motorist has a choice of two approaches to the mountain—you can arrive from Denver via Bergen Park and return via Idaho Springs or vice versa.

En route to the base of Mt. Evans, you'll pass large fertile meadows, dense lodgepole pine forests, aspen trees, ponderosa pine, Douglas fir, and thick bushes of wild raspberries; you can see chipmunks and squirrels.

You may want to stop at placid ◆ **Echo Lake,** where you'll notice families angling for trout, picnickers enjoying their lunch, or hikers setting out for the trails that captivated painter Bierstadt so many years ago. After Thanksgiving the lake freezes over completely. You can skate across it on your narrow cross-country skis and reach numerous trails that yield great views. Even in summer it gets cool up here, so dress warmly for the occasion. Indeed, scientists have established the theory that as you climb 1,000 feet in the Rockies, your upward journey can be compared to a 200-mile journey north, with the cooler air in each zone on the way up—and in each vegetation belt—to match. Spring, therefore, comes a little late. Above Echo Lake you wander through the tundra; you can study the small grasses, sedges, herbs, and the almost microscopic plants with miniflowers.

To be sure, the Mt. Evans drive can be an educational one, especially for children. If you take a close look at the ancient bristlecone pines, for instance, you will quickly understand that these and other trees must fight a fierce survival battle at these high altitudes.

Every dwarfed bristlecone or leaning Douglas fir up here tells a story of blizzards and summer storms, of blazing sunlight followed by rains. The weather destroys any exposed buds and conifer seeds, limiting their reproduction. Some trees are bent and twisted from the wind. The sun at these elevations bleaches trees; the lightning blackens and splits some of them. At timberline the little array of trees becomes sparse; there only single isolated soldiers face the sky's hail cannons.

Above timberline, in Colorado's Alpine Life Zone, you spy different animals, too. Marmot often show up, and occasionally ptarmigan birds; some people have even reported that bighorn sheep are common and that mountain goats may be seen near the summit. ("Don't feed them," advises the U.S. Forest Service. "They sometimes bite.")

The upper reaches of Mt. Evans are also dotted with lakes: At 11,700 feet you'll spot Lincoln Lake; it's 800 feet below the highway. Then at 12,830 feet Summit Lake awaits, complete with a short trail to overlook the picturesque Chicago Lakes, some 1,400 feet below. (The Forest Service warns parents not to let their kids run around too much, because of the sudden dropoffs. The highway has few guard rails.)

Finally, you can make your motorized conquest of the summit, at 14,264 feet, where the clouds may actually be below you, as they often are on airline flights. The final few feet are by trail. Catch your breath: The air is thinner than in the plains, of course, so flatland visitors would be wise to walk slowly and not to overexert themselves on the summit. You'll see a lot of Colorado from the top of Mt. Evans, and your children will talk about the sights for a long time afterward.

You can start your tour on I–70. Use exit 240 in Idaho Springs; then follow SR103 along Clear Creek to Echo Lake and SR5 to the Mt. Evans summit. For additional scenery and a change of pace, return to Denver via Squaw Pass Road and Bergen Park. The distances are moderate; it's just 28 miles from Idaho Springs, for example, to the summit of Mt. Evans.

A dude ranch vacation! What an unusual concept!

The horse trip leads to a sunny meadow full of wildflowers. A few ghost houses, with caved-in roofs and sagging walls, the wood evenly bleached by the sun. Later the party rides on. There is an excited breathlessness about the journey across two brooks, through thickets of willows and other bushes, then slowly down a steep, rocky slope. Caution and a touch of the primitive. The riders are in tune with the mountain and alone with their thoughts. It is quiet except for the slight creak of the leather saddles and the clicking of the hooves.

The vacationers are far away from the high rises and superhighways. The riders arrive for breakfast at a sunny forest clearing. Everyone sits down on long logs. The coffee steams. The cowboys fry eggs for all. The mountains say good morning.

Ask other travelers to share their experiences with you. They'll speak about the informality, the privacy, the utter friendliness of Colorado's guest ranches. What with an average of fifteen to about one hundred guests, the mood is calm and relaxed, and the owners really care about you. Families, couples, and newlyweds are pampered. If you arrive with a large party, you can write ahead for spacious quarters. At some hostelries you can also rent cabins.

The names say much: C Lazy U Ranch, Tumbling River Ranch, Peaceful Valley Dude Ranch. Endearing places in romantic isolated Colorado locations. Some of them still breed cattle or horses.

A Colorado dude ranch vacation is one of the most self-satisfying, genuine holidays available today. The air is clean, days are warm, evenings cool, and the mountain scenery absolutely spectacular.

At first primitive, the accommodations now range from rustic to deluxe ratings, such as Five Star by Mobil travel guides and Exceptional by AAA (American Automobile Association).

Colorado boasts well over fifty dude ranches, generally located in the scenic mountain regions. Activities are varied and informal. Life on the ranch resort is geared for the ultimate in easy relaxation. Guests are encouraged to set their own pace.

The essence of these cowboy-style vacations becomes clear when you read the greeting on a wall of one typical guest ranch on the Wyoming-Colorado border:

> *Guest, you are welcome here;*
> *Do as you please.*
> *Go to bed when you want to*
> *And get up at your ease.*
> *You don't have to thank us*
> *Or laugh at our jokes.*
> *Say what you like,*
> *You're one of the folks.*

You may ride all day every day or merely lounge by the heated pool and take in the pure mountain air. You don't even have to swim if you don't want to. Trail rides can be a few hours to half a day or full day with a picnic. Steak-fry rides are popular, too. At night the dudes head down a pine-scented trail in the moonlight; you gaze up at the Milky Way.

A Colorado dude ranch is a small, self-contained world where you ride away from city life as well. There are lots of horse trails for novices, guided breakfast rides, ghost town rides, and even six-day rides into the wilderness. Some dude ranches arrange river-rafting trips or you can rent a jeep. Archery, boating, and golf are common. Chaises abound.

The phenomenon is uniquely western and especially enjoyable in the Colorado mountains, where summers are never too hot or too cold. You're therefore outdoors much of the time. While adults rest or play, children have their own supervised programs. Much of the clientele returns every year. Most stay at least a week.

How much does a dude ranch vacation cost? Much less than you'd expect. If you settle on an average western place, you can have an unforgettable week for half or a third of what an ocean cruise would cost. Everything is included. Such vacations mean

Chapel at Peaceful Valley Dude Ranch

honest value; the customers can always rely on meals that are well cooked and served family style, which allows you to get acquainted with other guests. At one ranch, about a two-hour drive from Denver, the breakfasts and dinners consist of huge eat-all-you-want buffets. In the morning, you'll *want* to ride off some of those calories—and get some sun in the process.

At the large 130-guest Peaceful Valley Ranch in Lyons, you'll find a main lodge and many chalets, plus giant stables. Much of the heating comes from solar panels. And unexpectedly, the owners built an Austrian-style, onion-steepled church for guests. (The owners encourage churchgoing on Sunday morning, and they invite a pastor for the service. Weddings are also held here.)

The Peaceful Valley Ranch is best known for its summer square-dancing activities; the dude ranch employs a caller. This establishment has its own tennis court, a special teenage program, scout trips to ghost towns, and even English riding instruction. The rates are moderate here. Lyons is easy to reach from Denver via the Boulder Turnpike; then continue via SR7 and SR72. For more information: Star Route, Box 2811, Lyons 80540; (303) 747–2881.

The ◆ **Tumbling River Ranch** in Grant seems hewn out of native rock and local wood. At night you can hear the tumbling river under your window. The ranch stands at 9,200 feet above sea level, and, overhead, the stars stand out clearly. The ranch features not only horse activities but a handsome outdoor pool sheltered by glass panes. The food is excellent, and you get lots of personal attention from the owners, the Gordons.

Grant is a short trip southwest from Denver via US285. For more information: Tumbling River Ranch, Box 30, Grant 80448; (303) 838–5981 or (800) 654–8770.

And make a note of the Colorado Dude and Guest Ranch Association for more ranches: Box 300, Tabernash 80478; (303) 887–3128.

Listen to the story about an old Colorado stagecoach stop, bus stop, and tourist hub, which moved from a valley to a hillside, reluctant at first but grateful now. It is the story of the rebirth of Dillon, the town that had to make way for a giant new water supply reservoir—the pride of Denver. It also becomes the story of a vast recreational area two hours west of the state capital, an area amid forests of lodgepole pine, Engelmann spruce, and Douglas fir, a region larded with new picnic grounds, laced with Rocky Mountain flowers of all kinds, and graced with a 24½-mile lake shoreline.

Driving east on Highway 6, you see the man-made lake after you're out of the steep Glenwood Canyon, over Vail Pass, en route to Keystone. If your approach is from the east, you cross the 11,992-foot Continental Divide; then the highway suddenly straightens, and there it is—◆ **Lake Dillon.** On a summer day

31

the water can be a deep blue, dotted by white triangles of sails, and alive with small motorboats, cabin cruisers, and canoes skimming the surface. Now and then a fisherman angles for rainbow trout in good privacy.

From the beaches, beyond the encircling highways, the mountains sweep upward—the domain of climbers, hikers, and horseback riders. Streams are everywhere: Blue River, Snake River, Ten Mile Creek, all agleam in the sun. The much-needed waters splash across rocks into the reservoir, flowing toward Denver, through the unseen Roberts Tunnel, not far from Dillon.

The highway has two lanes here, and if you're in a hurry, you may well sweep past the sign that reads: DILLON, ELEVATION 9156. DENVER, 78 MILES.

The town is concealed by pines. But a surprise awaits the driver who heads into these woods. For all at once there is silence. The trucks rumbling toward Utah or Nebraska are no longer heard. And among the trees stands the new Dillon. The town fathers and the city planners conceived it well. Buildings can be no higher than 30 feet, for instance, so that all comers can see the lake. Only natural materials—the stone and wood of the Rockies plus glass—are permitted for the houses. The wood may be stained, not painted. The lots and homes have to keep their distance, for utmost peace. And timber was cut sparingly, for conservation's sake.

You notice other things. Dillon's signs are subdued, modest, inviting. Neon doesn't splash here; no beacons explode in the traveler's eyes. There are no unsightly shacks or dead auto carcasses. A cluster of stores—hardware, supermarket, drugs—and a post office have been fashioned into a tidy shopping center. Built of native pine, it blends with the forest.

The old town was named after an early prospector. There was off-and-on gold mining, a little railroading, lumber trading, and much ranching. The first post office opened here in 1883. With the advent of the car came garages and service stations. Roads improved, and more tourists showed up "to breathe the exhilarating Rocky Mountain air," as one man put it. A long-time resident remembers the Dillon of the thirties: "Ranchers picked up their mail here," he says, "and it was a place for a beer on Saturday night."

But on the other side of the mountains, Denver was growing, and it desperately needed more water. All through the forties and early fifties, the Denver Water Department bought up lands and ranches with water rights. Then, in 1955, Dillonites were told about the coming storage reservoir. It would inundate their town. This was a shock at first, but then some people spoke up. "Let us few have a heart for the many," said one man, meaning the water-hungry Colorado capital.

After many meetings and complex legal work, the machinery ground into high gear. There would be no turning back—Dillon had to move. Some of the old people left for warmer climates; others settled in nearby villages. But the young, sports-minded citizens decided to create a new Dillon on a hill of pine and evergreen. Here was a chance for a model town.

Down in the valley the old community was dismantled stick by stick. Because the water supply had to be pure, all the ancient buildings had to go. Some were cut in half and hauled elsewhere by trucks. Others had to be burned down. The water board uprooted telephone lines, removed old pipes, buried the last, rusty tin cans. Even the peaceful graveyard, with its rococo stones and metal crosses, had to be shifted to higher ground. For a while there were still the busy swings in the school yard, and a church belfry pointed its white wooden finger into the sky. Then the school was moved, and the church found a new home in the reborn Dillon.

Slowly, the dam rose until it stood 231 feet high at some points and was capable of backing up 257,000 acre-feet of water. The Harold Roberts Tunnel, more than 23 miles long and costing $50 million, was completed to connect the reservoir with rivers flowing into Denver. Water from thawing snows and the mountain streams steadily accumulated in the reservoir behind the dam. One August day the waters rushed over the top and through the "glory hole" spillway into the outlet tunnel. By then nothing was left of the old Dillon town site. The roads that led to it now lay under about 150 feet of water. Unlike the fabled Atlantis, the sunken island that resurfaces, the ancient Dillon would never emerge again.

Instead, the new town has forged quickly ahead. It is a community rooted in nature. The Ptarmigan, a lakeshore luxury motel, was named after a species of wild bird found in the peaks. The Arapahoe, a charming, wood-paneled minirestaurant, got its name from the surrounding forest land. A campground became the Alpine View. Dillon's tourists walk along a Buffalo Street.

Even nearby Summit County establishments, such as the Alpen-
top Deli and Spruce Sporting Goods, mirror the scenery.

This is sports country. On Memorial Day there is always a spectacular ◈ **Ski-and-Yachting Regatta.** Some of Dillon's bold
citizens soar downhill through colored flags on snow and then
navigate their boats along an obstacle course. Children, too, par-
take richly of snow, woods, and water. They ski for practically
nothing; they hunt with their fathers for elk and deer; they rush
outdoors with their fishing rods.

In the years ahead Dillon and the entire vacationland around
the 3,300-acre lake will witness even more development.
Involved are many agencies, including the U.S. Forest Service of
the Department of Agriculture, the Bureau of Land Management, the Denver Board of Water Commissioners, the Colorado
Game, Fish, and Parks Department, and, of course, the town of
Dillon itself. On the horizon are more motels, hotels, condos,
restaurants, clothing stores, curio and art shops, and perhaps a
"Think Center" for corporation executives and even a writing
seminar. The area expects many additional residents and vacationers, thanks to the interstate highway route through the
Continental Divide.

In summer Denver is a mere seventy driving minutes from
the lake and thirty more minutes from the booming resort town
of Vail.

Although capital is not always plentiful here, the townspeople are
full of enthusiasm about the future. This is best expressed in a recent
poster and auto bumper strip. It reads simply, THERE IS A DILLON!

For more information: Summit County Chamber, Box 214,
Frisco 80443; (303) 668–0376.

"Nearly impossible!" a geologist said when a Colorado financier
first suggested a long tunnel through the Continental Divide during the thirties. "Unpredictable rock!" other geologists warned
in 1941. The drilling of a pilot bore already gave a clue to the
unstable rock strata of the area in the Colorado Rockies. Steel
linings buckled in the exploratory shaft. For three decades tunnel
builders battled the mountain some 58 miles west of Denver.
Lack of money, politics, explosions, fires, and, most of all, geological problems all thwarted the builders. A tunnel engineer later
summed it up better than anyone else. "We were going by the
book," he said. "But the damned mountain couldn't read!"

Fortunately, the 8,941-foot-long ◈ **Eisenhower Tunnel** was eventually drilled despite the obstacles. The tunnel pierces Mount Trelease and saves the motorist 10 miles over the twisting and turning highway that crosses Loveland Pass. Since the tunnel opened in 1973, drivers need no longer expose themselves to the fierce storms and howling winds of the pass. No more jackknifed trucks, stranded cars, vehicles swept off the highway ledges by avalanches, rock slides, or icy curves taken too fast. One of North America's best-known mountain passes was finally tamed.

Its story is fascinating. For a hundred years, since the days when railroads were first reaching across the continent, men had worked and dreamed of tunneling through the Continental Divide here, where it's narrowest.

Everyone agreed that the existing roads across the 12,000-foot-high mountain crests presented some perils and inconveniences. In the twenties and thirties, a motor trip was still considered a major undertaking on the 12-foot-wide Loveland Pass road. The local papers claimed that such travel resembled a stunt and called the motorists undaunted. One eyewitness reported, "Mud and a steep grade combine to balk all but the highest built cars." In summer automobiles sometimes plummeted from the steep road, and hikers could see old hulks rusting in the valleys. The worst times were in winter, when Colorado's east and west slopes became cut off from each other. Eventually, irate citizens put placards on their auto bumpers that read, WE DEMAND A TUNNEL!

It became clear that only a tunnel would make travel possible at all seasons, besides reducing distances across the Rockies. In January 1937 a mountain community leader proposed a 10-mile tunnel. It took four years until the Colorado Highway Department began to drill a 5,483-foot pioneer bore. World War II brought the work to a halt, despite much clamor in the mountain towns and in the Colorado state capital. One November day in 1947, a large group of marchers showed up at the statehouse in Denver, calling for action. At the same time signs appeared in front range cafes and restaurants that demanded a LOVELAND PASS TUNNEL NOW!

Before long the tunnel idea moved into high gear. The project was advertised and bids were to be opened. Unfortunately, only one bid was received, which brought the tunnel idea to another standstill.

In short, the mountain giant had won. No one wanted to take it on. In the pilot bore the ceilings gradually caved in, and inspectors reported gushing water and musty odors. Engineers told the press that men would have to work and live under impossible climatic conditions at an 11,000-foot altitude and that it would be extremely difficult to transport materials to the site. Attention-seeking politicians showed up in the tunnel bore, garbed in yellow slickers, rubber boots, and impressive miner's hats. The test shaft's air quickly ended the visit.

During the early 1960s the tunnel reared its rocky head again; it found its way into the *Congressional Record*. "In a few years a tunnel will be carved through solid granite. It will be an engineering marvel."

Work progressed only slowly. The Continental Divide would not bow to the nine firms that had been welded into one contractor. Sometimes as many as 1,100 men sweated and coughed in three shifts inside the mountain. Mounted on three-tiered drilling platforms, a dozen giant drills poked into the tunnel's brain. The attack of these massive drilling machines was followed by blasts of water to wash out the fresh holes. The racket was tremendous, and bearded hard-hatted miners wore thick plastic earmuffs lined with sponge rubber.

After just three months of penetration, workmen noticed that a large area had shifted, buckling some steel linings. Total costs soon soared above the original bids of $49 million to $100 million, with the tunnel still acting up. On February 13, 1969, miners had to run for safety as some walls 600 feet inside the west portal started to disintegrate. Dismay was equally great when the granite resisted altogether. The contractor requested permission to attack one fault zone with a specially designed shield. The five-story, twelve-drill, 22-foot monster weighed 670 tons with its tailpiece. The machine was capable of exerting a push of twenty million pounds.

The shield was first housed in a mammoth chamber near the west portal. Came the historic day when the engineering wonder began its journey into the tunnel. The highway department's fanfare—and the newspapers' excitement—proved to be somewhat premature: The shield advanced only 70 feet in less than a month. On September 4, 1969, the device ground to a sudden standstill; its thirty-four roller bearings were stuck. The shield was redesigned to move on skids. This time, alas, the machine budged just 7 inches. The earth pressures were too much, and the expensive colossus had to be abandoned in the tunnel, where it still lies today, cemented into the walls.

No further progress was made for more than a year after this million-dollar failure. The tunnel designers brought in qualified consultants at stiff fees from all over the United States. To no avail. Finished sections still threatened to fall apart. On occasion the whole mass of granite, gneiss, and schist seemed to be moving. In some areas the rock resembled clay, and dust kept squeezing through every crevice. In the collapsing areas some rock could be "nailed" to a more stable surface; in other sections curved supports helped distribute the pressures. Sometimes the only solution was to double the support beams. All these unforeseen emergencies and the additional materials consumed a fortune in man-hours.

There were other problems. About sixty miners walked out when a woman was hired as an engineer. Twice the workmen walked out to protest poor ventilation.

One December day a fire brought work to a complete stop. No one knows for sure how the flames started some 4,000 feet inside the western tunnel section. An acetylene torch—and some straw—may have touched off the fire. To smother it the outside air supply had to be shut off, and the smoke assaulted the men's lungs. Would gas pockets cause an explosion? The possibility seemed real enough. Almost a week passed before work could continue.

Barely three months later a $200,000 explosion rocked the concrete operation at the west entrance. This time there may have been an equipment malfunction. The mishap destroyed the huge boiler, the concrete-mixing machinery, 5,000 gallons of oil, a large propane tank, and the company ambulance.

The job had been enormous on all levels: The excavation alone had taken 524,000 cubic yards out of a mountain bent on creating mischief and causing deaths. The tunnel actually took five lives—three in accidents, two from heart attacks at the high elevation. There were more than fifty broken arms, legs, and ankles. No one could count the hours of anguish felt by the contractors, engineers, and workmen about whether the job would ever get finished. The mountain giant constantly held out its fist for more money. The original highway department estimate—made in 1937—was $1 million. The cost exceeded $115 million for one bore.

Yet all this effort and expenditure represented a mere start, because the tunnel could at first accommodate only one lane of traffic each way. The interstate highway system must be four lanes, so a second section was dug by some 500 workers at a cost of another $225 million. The complete Eisenhower Tunnel opened for traffic on December 21, 1979. Lots of bad rock gave the engineers and drilling crews plenty of trouble.

But the job was at last accomplished. "The damned mountain finally knew the score," said one engineer. "Like it or not, we *did* get through!"

The Eisenhower Tunnel is 58 miles west of Denver via I–70.

YEAR-ROUND VACATION AREAS

◆ **Breckenridge** is the perfect little Colorado frontier town—one of the few that was rebuilt and is now well preserved and thriving.

When a group of European journalists visited many of the state's resorts, Breckenridge seemed to delight them more than most others. Why? Here were all the earmarks of the Old Gold Rush West: the little Victorian houses with their columns and crenellations; the clapboard structures of the miners, beautifully repainted; and store windows filled with antiques. Midwesterners and easterners feel the same way; they get the chance to let children relive U.S. history.

The ski slopes are still named for the old mines in the area: Gold King, Wellington, Bonanza, Cashier, Silverthorn—these were the names that excited the gold hunters more than a century ago.

Breckenridge is actually one of Colorado's oldest towns. In August 1859 the first gold-seekers came streaming across the Continental Divide to pan gold in the waters of the Blue River. Later a silver lode started a second boom.

By 1861 some 5,000 people lived in and near Breckenridge. Summit County then extended as far as the Utah line and was one of seventeen counties composing Colorado Territory. It has since been whittled down to 615 square miles. Then, as now, Breckenridge was the county seat.

Breckenridge

More than $30 million in gold was taken out of the district during its heyday. Most of that was from placer and lode mining. Later on gold dredges came to tear up the countryside, leaving the great piles of rocks still to be seen along the Blue and Swan rivers, as well as along French Creek. Dredging came to a halt about 1942.

In the early 1960s Breckenridge became a year-round resort, at the same time maintaining its century-old status as a former mining community.

Development moved ahead when the ski area opened in the early sixties. The runs were at first short but fairly varied and always aimed at families who could meet for lunch at the handsome Alpine base lodge. Soon the town attracted a number of good people who built second homes in the serene forests.

Breckenridge is a good choice for the family in search of a winter vacation without pretense: snowmobiling, ice fishing, easy skiing on the simply laid-out ski runs, tobogganing, snowshoeing, bowling, sightseeing. Rates here are expensive, but most ski resorts are in this state.

To amuse the tourists, a yearly Pack Burro Race takes place at the end of July from Fairplay over Mosquito Pass to Leadville. In this world championship race, contestants run alongside their loaded burros for about four hours, going 26 miles up hill and dale. Entry rules? "No needles, electric prods, narcotics, clubs or whips. No firearms. No riding of burros, but running alongside instead."

Breckenridge is 88 miles west of Denver via I–70 and SR9. For more information: Breckenridge Resort Chamber, P.O. Box 1909, Breckenridge 80424; (303) 453–6018 or (800) 221–1901.

A ski museum? Yes, Colorado's only one and one of the few such historical gathering places in the United States. Founded in 1976, the ◆**Colorado Ski Museum** reaches back to the old miners of the last century who raced in the Rockies surrounding their camps, competing against one another on long wooden boards, holding a long staff in one fist for braking. The museum contains a magnificent, enlarged 1859 etching of Snowshoe Thompson, the Norwegian who skied from camp to camp in severe blizzards. He delivered the mails, candy, and medicines to the marooned miners.

Here are the photos and artifacts of skiing clergymen like Father John Lewis Dyer, who brought the gospel to Colorado's historic gold towns, as well as the stories of sheepherders and trappers who braved the snows in the nineteenth century on 9-foot enormous wooden contraptions with crude leather straps holding their boots. (Some of the men used baling wire to keep the ski shovel curved during summer storage.) Mementos of the first long-ago jumpers will fascinate the viewers; photos show them taking off from knolls or flying through the air, equipment sometimes falling off meters above ground.

Do you want to learn more about the first ski lifts? The Colorado Ski Museum displays the drive mechanism, pictures of the first rope tows, and photos of funny "grippers," which latched onto the moving ropes. The localized history of chairlifts, gondolas (including a gondola rescue), ski patrol toboggans, the first U.S. Army Snow Tanks, and the first ski area snow-packing and grading gear can all be seen here. Any student of ski equipment can learn much about the development of skis, bindings, boots, poles, even the first ski suits, knickerbockers, parkas, or the women's fashions of still earlier days when ladies skied in black skirts to the ankles.

The history of Colorado's famous Tenth Mountain Division is well illustrated; indeed, an entire room is devoted to the Mountain Troopers and their initial camps and wartime exploits. If the viewer is curious about methods of avalanche fighting or up-to-date ski racing or the history of plush, urban, expensive Vail, it's all here in the very center of Vail, next door to the sleek bank, a few steps from the five-star Lodge at Vail, and near the ski slopes themselves. The museum now features ski videos in the video viewing area. And plaques contain the pictures and biographies of Colorado Ski Hall of Fame members—a somewhat politicized assembly of engineers and entrepreneurs, ski makers and ski teachers.

The museum charges a small fee, except during October and November up to Thanksgiving, when admission is free. Open daily 10:00 A.M.–5:00 P.M. except Mondays; closed during the slow May and October seasons, except on some weekends. Colorado Ski Heritage Museum, 231 South Frontage Road East, Vail Village Transportation Center, Vail 81658; (303) 476–1876.

Within walking distance of the ski museum—but nicely concealed by a thick grove of fir trees—you'll find the beautifully designed ❖ **Vail Public Library.** It was built in 1972 with native Colorado stone and woods and a grass lawn roof. A massive fireplace is lit all year. Picture windows look out into the little forest and onto the footpath that meanders along Gore Creek to Vail Village.

Pam Hopkins, the young local architect, won all kinds of design awards for the building. "We wanted light and endless space," she explains. "Yet we aimed for energy efficiency." The library has some 23,000 volumes, including many mountain books; several hundred magazine subscriptions; an eager reference desk department; plus cassettes and a children's department. Most of all, the building feels especially cosy when rain or snow glistens in the needles of the trees outside while you're warm and dry, book in hand. Library hours are 9:00 A.M. to 9:00 P.M. daily, except Sunday, when the doors open at 1:00 and close at 5:00 P.M. For more information: 292 West Meadow, Vail 81657; (303) 479–2183.

Two hours west of Denver, in some of the state's most impressive mountains, is the ◆ **Gore Range.** In Vail itself you'll see the Gore Creek, especially in summer. Gore Mountain, Gore Wilderness—who in the world was Gore?

You might call him one of the most interesting visitors who ever roamed through Colorado. The best way to get acquainted with him might be on Gore Pass. Here a bronze plaque is visible beside the highway, at an elevation of 9,000 feet. The words on the bronze may pique your curiosity:

> HERE IN 1854 CROSSED SIR ST. GEORGE GORE, AN IRISH BARONET BENT ON SLAUGHTER OF GAME AND GUIDED BY JIM BRIDGER. FOR THREE YEARS HE SCOURED COLORADO, MONTANA AND WYOMING ACCOMPANIED USUALLY BY FORTY MEN, MANY CARTS, WAGONS, HOUNDS AND UNEXAMPLED CAMP LUXURIES.

Lord Gore's party, we learn, dispatched "more than 2000 buffalo, 1600 elk and deer, and 100 bears," among others.

Hunting was nothing new in a land where European trappers and fur traders had already searched all of Colorado for beaver. But Lord Gore set a record; besides, no one matched his style. The baronet had brought most of his retinue of hunters and even some porters from Ireland; his safari caravan eventually accumulated 112 horses, twenty-one carts, thirty wagons and four dozen hunting dogs. He roamed the mountains for many months, shooting grizzly bear, antelope, and other animals and making elegant camp at night, complete with silver service and rare wines.

His Lordship could afford the "unexampled camp luxuries." For one thing, his income exceeded $200,000, which was quite a sum during the mid-1850s. For another, the Irish nobleman had a taste for gourmet cuisine and rare wines—and the cooks and servants to attend his needs. Lord Gore had gone to school in Oxford, and his aristocratic tastes included various mansions in Ireland and houses in East Sussex.

Lord Gore's hunt is still spoken of by schoolchildren in the area. And thanks to the Historical Society of Colorado, future visitors to the region will be reminded of the Irishman and his exploits by means of the bronze plaque.

The summit of Gore Pass and the plaque are 17 miles west of

Kremmling and can be reached from Denver via US40. The Forest Service has provided picnic grounds on the pass. Vail can be reached by driving south on SR9, then west on I–70.

Mountain flowers! What a variety of life forms! Botanists estimate that there are some 6,000 species in the Rockies alone. Who can doubt it?

Just go to the Colorado foothills and then higher up, repeating your hikes each month. What a myriad of colors! Lavender, crimson, blue brushstrokes! Bright white, butter yellow, pink! The first sign of spring brings forth a rush of Easter daisies, mountain marigolds, wild sweetpeas, fairy trumpets, pink rockhill phlox, and others in many hues. Wander up in early summer to Colorado's 8,000- or 9,000-foot levels. And lo! Here, almost overnight, you'll see leafy cinquefoils, arnicas, yellow monkey flowers, and the official state flower, the blue Rocky Mountain columbine. (The latter also grows in the foothills.) In July you'll be welcomed by the star gentians, wood lilies, the mountain aster, and several kinds of larkspur.

You cannot help but admire the hardiness of vegetation at the altitudes of the Rockies. How is it possible that the plants do not die under the battle conditions of winter storms? What makes tiny wildflowers get along with less oxygen and more radiation? How do some mountain flowers manage to spite the short summers and harsh climate above timberline? A sense of wonder must fill you at some mountaintop discoveries.

First of all, smallness helps. The tinier the leaves, the less resistance to the wind. In the summit meadows, known as tundra, you will discover miniature grasses, sedges, and herbs. You bend down to miniflowers. If you brought a magnifying glass, you'd see details of almost microscopic leaves. There are plants without any stems; others come with stems so short that the swirling air masses can't budge them. At the same time the roots go deep down into the ground; a 2-foot root is the 2-inch plant's insurance against being ripped out by storms.

Amazing nature! Most mountain flora hold onto the day's warmth at night by closing their petals.

Mountain flowers protect themselves with tiny umbrellas or hairs, fine layers of wool, or waxy leaves that hold moisture. Mountain flowers can also adapt to the cold. In the Rockies thousands of avalanche lilies push through the snow, thus surprising the traveler with their delicate (and edible) yellow petals.

The growing season is short in Colorado. And nature has wisely arranged for most mountain flowers to be perennials so that they need not struggle each season. Such flora develop slowly but survive for several years. Other wildflowers sprout for a brief period at certain months each year. They thrive and shine under mysterious direction of sun and season, in concert with the flora elsewhere, waiting and then multiplying.

One Swiss botanist, Fritz Egli, notes the wondrous cycle of those multiplying and then vanishing creations: "Storms sweep up the seeds, blow them away, and wherever they fall—sometimes in the most inauspicious places—a tiny new life tries to take root; just one little life, inconspicuous among millions and millions more. Yet this tiny plant clings, waits, grows, and—bringing forth flower, color, and fruit—to master all the adversities."

Visitors to the Vail area shouldn't miss seeing the highest public alpine gardens in North America—◆ **The Betty Ford Alpine Gardens,** located at the Gerald Ford Park. The dedication took place in August 1989, in the presence of the former First Lady.

At an elevation of 8,200 feet, tourists encounter a profusion of crocus, heather, forsythia, wild roses, and other perennial mountain plants, shrubs, and trees. A total of 500 different varieties of alpine and subalpine plants grow in four separate microclimates.

There is no charge to visit the gardens, but donations are accepted. For more information: Betty Ford Alpine Gardens, 183 Gore Creek Drive, Vail 81657; (303) 476–0103.

As the vacation season grinds into high gear, park personnel gird themselves for millions of summer motorists, campers, hikers, climbers, backpackers, and other visitors. Every year travelers flock in record numbers to Colorado.

Can anything be done to lessen the impact on the fragile environment? The answer is yes.

As a traveler, you can do much to improve the situation in the Colorado mountains. Begin by not picking wildflowers. (In Switzerland tourists pay a heavy fine if they're caught gathering edelweiss and some other rare species.)

Continue by not littering. Apparently, one litterer creates another. Many local mountain clubs organize hikes for volunteer crews to pick up trash on or near hiking trails. In Estes Park the owners of a resort periodically ride up the trails on pack horses with saddlebags to pick up empty cigarette packages and candy wrappers. At the nearby YMCA mountain guides pick up the empty beer cans of the careless Sunday masses.

The head of a Colorado environment group says: "Some tourists are poor stewards of the Beautiful Country. They drive spikes into trees, use privies for target practice, shatter the forest stillness with radio or TV set. They leave initials in red paint on the rock face."

Hikers can help prevent erosion by not getting off the trail. (The state is blessed with more than 1,000 walking trails, footpaths, and mountain-bike routes.) It's especially important to stay on the paths in the high-altitude "tundra" areas. The flowers and vegetation are fragile.

Please, refrain from cutting your initials into trees, a rather common and brutal practice.

If you happen to visit a western ghost town this summer, take nothing but photographs. Forget about carrying off a souvenir piece of an abandoned cabin. Future visitors will be grateful to view the complete ghost town.

The environment credo should also interest people who toss bottle caps into resort streams. Please don't. The cap may get stuck in a fish's throat. One final good rule: If you carry it in, carry it out.

Lastly, one local conservationist suggests that the state adopt a slogan that warns, "There is only *one* Colorado. Tread gently. Make it last!"

What is one of the most unforgettable sights and experiences in this tourist-happy state? It's the 2-block-long ◆ **Glenwood Hot Springs** with happy heads of visitors bobbing in the steam, adults doing their hydrotherapy, small children riding rubber ducks, and—lo!—high mountains on all sides. Surrounded by the Rockies, with views of conifers and meadows, these thermal waters *are* relaxing. The Ute Indians discovered them and spoke of "miraculous healing powers." The Aspen, Colorado, mining king used these hot springs for relaxation. A famed architect, imported from Vienna, Austria, built the bathhouses here in 1890, and soon assorted American presidents came to visit Glenwood's mineral spa and "Natatorium."

Today the recreational, swimming—and walking—part is kept at 85 to 95°F (29 to 32°C); hotter outdoor waters (100 to 104°F, 38 to 40°C) are also available, fed more than 3½ million gallons. Swimmers relish the almost unlimited space in the pool, while former hospital patients or the temporarily lame—like skiers

45

recuperating from broken legs—enjoy the medical benefits. To be sure, scientists point out that the hot springs contain cornucopia elements, including magnesium, calcium, sulphates, bicarbonates, phosphates, and silica.

Some travelers recline much of the day in deck chairs around the 2-block-long pool—Colorado's version of the *dolce vita.* No Roman bath could match Glenwood's pure air and mountain views, however. For extra luxury the nearby vapor baths feature massages, plus natural saunas.

Glenwood Springs may be one of the state's more interesting communities—historically, economically, scenically—yet it never gets the kind of attention accorded to Aspen (41 miles to the southeast) or overcrowded, overbuilt Vail (59 miles) or Denver, some 158 miles to the east. Buses, rental cars—and even Amtrak trains—connect travelers daily from the Colorado state capital with Glenwood. To reach it from Denver, you use busy I-70 through Glenwood Canyon, which, steep rock walls, Colorado River, and all, reminds you of a narrow Grand Canyon. Unfortunately, and controversially, a segment of the interstate has been widened; man intruded on mountains.

Glenwood Springs is the gateway to some of Colorado's most dramatic and most photographed peaks, like the Maroon Bells near Snowmass, or lone, spectacular Mt. Sopris, which you notice from almost everywhere in the region. The immense ◆**White River National Forest** offers backpackers much wilderness. Fishermen rave about the catches of trout (rainbows or browns) in the surrounding rivers—the Roaring Fork, the Frying Pan, and the Colorado. Glenwood has guides that take you rafting and kayaking. And hiking possibilities are plentiful. Hunters come to the region for elk, deer, grouse, and waterfowl. Head for the ◆**Hanging Lake** trail, complete with waterfall; it's one of the local favorites.

Nine miles east of Glenwood on I-70, the 1$\frac{2}{10}$-mile trail to Hanging Lake is a peaceful respite after long hours on the interstate. The lure of this steep hike is the lush green foliage near the creek; the impressive redstone canyon walls; the gushing power of Deadhorse Creek; and, finally, the lake itself. A perfect gem.

Formed by a geological fault that caused the lake floor to drop down the canyon wall, Hanging Lake covers more than an acre and is up to 25 feet deep. Handrails near the top of the path provide welcome help on a steep grade. A boardwalk circles part of the lake. It crosses waterfalls crashing down from the cliff face. The summer mist from the falls is cooling. Autumn adds gilded accents as quaking golden aspen mix with pines. Icicles line the lake in winter and frozen formations stimulate the imagination. Hanging Lake is a great side trip any time of year.

Both town and area are blessed with accommodations for every pocketbook. Economy travelers welcome the numerous camp-grounds or inexpensive little cabins flanking the soothing rivers. Large and small motels abound.

You're never far from the parades with floats, carnivals, and other festivities of Glenwood's ❖ **Strawberry Days,** yearly fishing contests, various rodeos, the ❖ **Fall Art Festival,** and the quiet mountain paths under a blue sky.

Strawberry Days, now almost one hundred years old, is Glenwood Spring's oldest and most beloved annual event. The festival is thought to be Colorado's oldest civic celebration, dating back to 1898.

Early Glenwood Springs residents loved parties, and nearly everything called for a celebration. Prior to 1898 strawberry picnics celebrated the luscious harvest of berries that farmers grew in nearby fields.

Neighboring towns were first invited to the party in 1898, which was the advent of the first annual Strawberry Days. Special guest trains from Aspen, Leadville, and Grand Junction brought party-goers from throughout the region.

The event was a phenomenal success, growing in attendance and extravagance every year. In 1905 it was estimated that more than 6,000 out-of-town guests plus the residents of Glenwood Springs took part in the festivities. Aside from enjoying the delicious harvest, other activities included competition for the biggest strawberry, swimming in the Natatorium, a parade of floats and brass bands along Grand Avenue, and dancing in the streets.

Today many aspects of the original Strawberry Days remain. Free strawberries and ice cream are still enjoyed by all in Sayre "Strawberry" Park following the parade of floats and marching bands on Grand Avenue. There are still picnicking and dancing in the park as well.

The celebration has also been extended by several days, and

many new activities—including sporting events, kids' events, top-name entertainment, and an Artisan's Fair—have been added.

The Artisan's Fair features American hand-crafted work, with the majority of the artisans residing in Colorado. Attendance at the fair has risen to an estimated 30,000 people over the peak weekend.

Each year a new theme is chosen for the festival. The 1993 prevailing theme, "Moon over the Wild Strawberries," had Native American overtones, deriving from the Seneca Indian word for the month of June, which translates to mean "Moon When the Wild Strawberries Get Ripe."

The celebration is usually held in mid-June.

The Fall Art Festival, held the fourth week in September, is one of the largest art shows on the Western Slope, attracting more than 400 entries. Professionals and amateurs all compete in their own levels and media. And, of course, almost everything is for sale after the judging.

And to be sure, your hotel or inn will never be far from Glenwood Springs's famous year-round outdoor pool—a thermal wonder that doesn't force you to *swim;* you can just walk through most of it, for your health's sake.

It all adds up to quite a vacation destination.

Luckily, pool guests nowadays have a place to stay; in fact, they can see the steaming waters right under their windows. The 107-unit ◆ **Hot Springs Lodge** is contemporary, bright, efficient, and ideally located. Rates are moderate. For reservations write 415 Sixth Street, Glenwood Springs 81602, or call (800) 537–7946.

Perhaps you prefer more intimate, off-the-beaten-path accommodations. While the Hot Springs Lodge overlooks the famed pool, the scarcely known ◆ **Kaiser House** serves as a bed-and-breakfast in the quiet residential area of Glenwood Springs. It's a charmer, a gem. The owners are perfectionists; they keep the six bedrooms extra tidy. The little inn wouldn't be listed here were it not so perfectly Victorian, with dormers and gabled windows, triangular and circular roofs, and little verandahs up front. Inside you'll find lots of genuine antiques. The atmosphere is congenial. Good breakfast; no smoking. Location? Not far from Glenwood Springs's Main Street, with its hardware store and western wear shop that rents skis, too.

Write or call: Kaiser House, 932 Cooper Avenue, Glenwood Springs 81601; (303) 945–8827.

Other "Glenwood" leads: Chamber Resort Association, 1102

Grand Avenue, Glenwood Springs 81601; (303) 945–6589 or (800) 221–0098. The community is easy to reach from Denver by rental car, bus, or train. Motorists use I–70. The distance to Denver is 158 miles.

While you're in Glenwood Springs, don't fail to take a leisurely stroll through the stately ◆ **Hotel Colorado,** which graces the National Register of Historic Places. The 128-room hotel is one of the oldest in the state. Indeed, it was modeled after Italy's Villa Medici and boasts a Florentine fountain in a landscaped courtyard. The hotel's renovated beige lobby must be one of the most attractive in the western United States. The myriad chandeliers, fireplaces, oil paintings, and potted palm trees hark back to the days of Royalty and the Very Rich.

The Hotel Colorado was actually financed by the silver mining of the nearby Aspen region and opened officially on June 10, 1893. The cost was a horrendous $850,000; some sixteen private railroad cars of the industrial barons drew up on a special Glenwood siding. Leading citizens from all over the world registered. European millionaires arrived in droves to stay and dine here. In 1905 President Theodore Roosevelt brought his own appetite; a typical menu encouraged the presidential visitor and his entourage to consume an eight-course repast:

>*Caviar Canapés*
>*Consommé Rothschild*
>*Veal Sweetbreads*
>*Young Turkey*
>*Spring Lamb*
>*Broiled Squab*
>*Figs*
>*Roquefort Cheese*

Actually, Roosevelt—an avid bear hunter—made the hotel his Spring White House, complete with direct telegraph connections to Washington and special couriers bringing international news to the hunting head of state.

"The Marvel of Hoteldom" attracted the likes of the Armours of packinghouse fame; the "Unsinkable" Molly Brown, who managed to survive the *Titanic*'s sinking; and President William Howard Taft, who appeared to address the local populace during his term. World War II transformed the hotel into a naval hospital. In more recent times moneys were spent to update the facilities, to repair

49

leaking roofs and stalled elevators or failing steam heat. Thanks to their antiques, several suites are reminiscent of yesteryear's elegant clientele.

For more information and reservations: Hotel Colorado, 526 Pine, Glenwood Springs 81601; (303) 945–6511.

Even by Colorado standards, the trip to Redstone is long and complicated, but it is worth it. The distance only enhances the charms of the little hamlet of Redstone and its historic inn and castle.

You at once see the imposing ❖**Redstone Inn** at the end of the main street. The Tudor clock tower is an unexpected sight in this remote mountain landscape. The thirty-five rooms seem cozy and unpretentious. Rates are moderate. The lobby and the restaurant are filled with antiques and a Victorian atmosphere.

Now on the National Register of Historic Places, the small Redstone hostelry was built in 1902 for unmarried coal miners. The building had steam heat and even a barber shop. Later more than $1 million was invested in hotel facilities. A stay here, at an elevation of 7,200 feet, means pure air and a true escape from the city. In summer horses are for rent; trout fishing is popular. The Crystal River is quiet and lovely. Hikers enjoy the area, as do backpackers. In winter the inn serves as headquarters for cross-country skiing. Call (303) 963–2526 or (800) 748–2524.

One mile away you'll see ❖**Cleveholm Manor** (the Historic Redstone Castle), 58 Redstone Boulevard; (303) 963–3463. It began in 1900 as the home of mining baron J. C. Osgood, whose Fuel and Iron Company made him a millionaire. Osgood had extravagant tastes: His $2.5 million "Cleveholm Manor" ceilings were covered with gold leaf; his furnishings were embellished with silk brocade and imported ruby velvet. The baronial opulence included elegant chandeliers and expensive Oriental carpets. He built coachman's quarters, a carriage house, and elaborate stables.

Osgood's manor has forty-two rooms, fourteen fireplaces, oak paneling, assorted red turrets, dormers, and terraces; it is surrounded by its own golf course and 450 acres of mountain land. Osgood and a succession of wives enjoyed entertaining industrialists and celebrities of his times. Today you can view the manor by joining a scheduled tour or by renting a room through their bed and breakfast; private weddings and parties are held here, too. Phone: (303) 963–3463.

The little hamlet of Redstone is idyllic. Just a few houses, some artisan and gift shops, a cafe, and a general store.

You reach Redstone via I–70 west to Glenwood Springs, then SR82 south out of Glenwood toward Aspen; turn right at Carbondale on SR133—it's 18 miles to Redstone.

The chairs whir upward over forest spurs and logging roads and enormous ravines that become expert ski runs in winter. From "downtown" Aspen one can see just a small portion of the whole Aspen Mountain; in fact, only a third of it is visible to those who merely stare up from their cars.

Aspen called itself at first Ute City because it was in Ute territory. Silver gave the town its big start, back in the early 1880s. The first news made the prospectors head up the passes and rush to Aspen. A hard, punishing journey, even from nearby Leadville. Some men dropped dead before they could stake their first claim. Western historians still mention the stampede of that winter in 1879. They came on burro, on foot, or on horseback. A man would sometimes keel over and die on the Aspen street. Other prospectors just stuck the body into a snowbank and kept up the frantic search for silver riches. The best years were from 1885 to 1889, when mines galore—some with fascinating names like The Smuggler or Montezuma—operated above the mountain town. The smelter was booked for weeks, and silver rock would pile up everywhere. Some miners got rich fast. "The men filled their pockets and fled," wrote one contemporary. The silver barons built the luxurious Victorian ◆ **Hotel Jerome,** and an opera house. They imported singers and musicians from Vienna and dainty furniture from Paris.

The crash came in 1893, however, and brought lean times. Aspen shriveled from a population of 13,000 to a mere 500. The rebirth followed in the thirties, with skiing.

Old mining equipment was used as the first tow. After World War II Chicago industrialist Walter Paepcke became interested in Aspen as a cultural and sports colony. The pace accelerated in the little mountain town. Paepcke made good use of the granitic old opera house, and the guests were housed in the Jerome Hotel, which had been built in 1889. The Aspen Music School flourished.

Some of the townspeople, however, didn't go along with the Chicagoan. When Paepcke offered them free paint for their shacks, not many old-timers took him up on it. They didn't like

51

Fishing near Aspen, Colorado

outsiders and wanted to be left alone. One former prospector complained to the papers that it was a "tragedy to reduce a once-great mining camp to a mere Tenderfoot Playground." Another wrote: "Gallons of printers ink to lure the tourist! And not a drop of ink to tell the world where we stood, back in the eighties shouting to the very top of Castle Peak: 'Here's the greatest ore deposit in North America!'"

In the late 1940s many Aspen dwellings were peeling. Some stood empty. But the mountain town had uniformity. The residences and streets formed a near-perfect grid pattern. If one studies the town from Aspen Mountain, there was—and still is—a simplicity to it.

The aerial view is about the same even today. Closer inspection, however, reveals some architectural mix. Free enterprise!

Aspen rediscovered as the former mining community grew into a 10,000-tourist-bed complex, which has meanwhile doubled.

No one seemed to agree on architectural styles, and every year downtown Aspen looked more citylike. There were the original log cabins and Victorian homes of the early miners. Contractors moved in to build new "mineshaft" condominiums, some of which block mountain views. In the more than forty years' development, Aspen may have retained some flaws, but it also succeeded beyond all expectations as a resort. The ski facilities, what with four different ski areas and countless lifts, including the rapid Silver Creek gondola, are all extraordinary, as good as anything in Europe. Aspen summers are a delight, with classical music, lectures, meetings, trails for hikers and bikers, rivers for anglers, areas for kiters, and an expanded airport for private pilots. Gourmets flock to the mostly overpriced Aspen restaurants; finicky guests check into ultra-expensive new hotels. And on Red Mountain, where the movie stars live, the parties go on every night.

Because of the seasonal rush, some little-known accommodations can be recommended. Try the Condominium Rental Management (747 South Galena Street, Aspen 81611; 800–321–7025) for otherwise hard-to-get lodging.

The scene is a Saturday morning in Ashcroft, a remote Colorado ghost town near Aspen. The first sun rays redden the snow. The base of nearby Castle Peak is still mauve. Nothing seems to stir in this winter landscape. Then complete daylight, bright, golden, topped by the flawless Colorado sky.

A few human figures assemble down the road from Ashcroft's weather-beaten buildings. Quietly, more people arrive, get together, wait for still others. All carry snowshoes, which will permit an unhurried penetration of this backcountry.

By 9:00 A.M. forty snowshoers stand ready, almost twice as many as the Colorado Mountain Club leader had expected.

Why is old-fashioned snowshoeing in again? The reasons are easy to understand. For one thing, snowshoeing is just winter hiking. You don't need any lessons; you learn to walk with your webbed contraptions in minutes. Age is no factor, and women do just as well as men. Snowshoeing is healthy; that's why you find many doctors devoted to it.

A sports medicine committee of the American Academy of Surgeons made a study of energy output in various sports. According

*The following mountains are Colorado's fourteeners—
peaks that are 14,000 feet or higher.*

Mt. Elbert	14,433	Mt. Sneffels	14,150
Mt. Massive	14,421	Mt. Democrat	14,148
Mt. Harvard	14,420	Capitol Peak	14,130
Blanca Peak	14,345	Pikes Peak	14,110
LaPlata Peak	14,336	Snowmass Mountain	14,092
Uncompahgre Peak	14,309	Mt. Eolus	14,084
Crestone Peak	14,294	Windom Peak	14,082
Mt. Lincoln	14,286	Challenger Point	14,080
Grays Peak	14,270	Mt. Columbia	14,073
Mt. Antero	14,269	Culebra Peak	14,069
Torreys Peak	14,267	Missouri Mountain	14,067
Castle Peak	14,265	Humboldt Peak	14,064
Quandary Peak	14,265	Mt. Bierstadt	14,060
Mt. Evans	14,264	Sunlight Peak	14,059
Longs Peak	14,255	Handies Peak	14,048
Mt. Wilson	14,246	Mt. Lindsey	14,042
Mt. Cameron	14,239	Ellingwood Point	14,042
Mt. Shavano	14,229	Little Bear Peak	14,037
Mt. Princeton	14,197	Mt. Sherman	14,036
Mt. Belford	14,197	Red Cloud Peak	14,034
Mt. Yale	14,196	Pyramid Peak	14,018
Crestone Needle	14,191	Wilson Peak	14,017
Mt. Bross	14,172	Wetterhorn Peak	14,017
Kit Carson Peak	14,165	North Maroon Peak	14,014
El Diente Peak	14,159	San Luis Peak	14,014
Maroon Peak	14,156	Huron Peak	14,005
Tabeguache Mountain	14,155	Mt. of the Holy Cross	14,005
Mt. Oxford	14,153	Sunshine Peak	14,001

to one of the cardiologists, snowshoeing proved exceptionally good for the heart. The energy expenditure is at a safe level. Besides, you can rest during the trip and survey the scenery. For all ages this sport means a better workout for heart and lungs, better muscle tone, better-functioning organs, better digestion, and better circulation.

Cardiologists will tell you that leg veins have valves to maintain circulation. Good muscle tone helps squeeze these veins. The valves permit the blood to go one way, back toward the heart. The better the tone of the leg muscles, the better the circulation, the less work the heart has to do. Vigorous use of the legs is important whether it is walking, bicycling, skiing, snowshoeing, or any other exercise that uses the legs.

You can go almost anywhere on snowshoes: up the steep winter meadows of the Continental Divide, across the gentle mounds of eastern Colorado, over frozen Lake Dillon, in the dramatic deep-snow regions above Silverton and Ouray. In a survey made by the Sierra Club (which has an active snowshoe chapter), some members explained their own special motivations: "We don't disturb nature on snowshoes. We don't upset ecology."

That's what makes the sport different from skiing, especially the kind done at resorts. Colorado's snowshoers demand no cuttings of trees, no bulldozing of ski boulevards, no base lodges noisy with hard-rock music. Modern ski complexes resemble mechanized cities, with lifts of all kinds, $42 ticket prices, and long lines of waiting customers. By contrast, snowshoers never have to stand in a queue; they can move whenever they please and stay warm in the process. Most skiing is now a status symbol; fashion is absent from snowshoeing.

You need only be warm. You can therefore dress in your oldest sweater, the most beat-up windbreaker, a plain cap, an ancient faded sports shirt; no one will judge your income from the pants, either. Any kind of boot will do, including the kind used for hiking.

All this drives down the cost.

Snowshoe equipment is astonishingly reasonable. In a major city like Denver, for instance, you can *rent* a good pair of shoes with harness. What's the charge for the weekend? Ten dollars per day for adult sizes. At an average retail store, you can buy a pair of new snowshoes for a reasonable price.

It's a fairly simple matter to choose a pair of snowshoes. The shape and material may vary, but all the shoes consist of a frame connected to some lacing. The binding is uncomplicated.

Unless you're in first-rate shape, a first trip will mean some muscle pains. Snowshoes can weigh several pounds, and every step means a workout for your legs. As you start out, the shoes feel awkward, and it will take fifteen minutes until you get used to the wide stance required for walking. (If you step normally, your own legs will be in the way.) You'll eventually learn to raise your feet as little as possible, and after half a mile you won't step on top of your own shoes. But unlike skiing, where you must become familiar with the technique, snowshoeing requires mostly good legs. If the snow is right, you can use your leg strength—and body weight—for excellent snowshoe descents.

"The scenic rewards are great," says one enthusiast of the West. "All evidence of man is swept under a deep, sound-absorbing blanket of white. Each pine cone, every spruce branch stand out clearly. Nature is always there."

The rapid ski lift purrs you upward to 9,000 feet, 10,000, 11,000. At 11,500 you slide off your perch and cross the clearing to a vantage point. You have done it before. But each time you catch your breath. The sight is stunning. The white surface ripples downward to your left and right, agleam in the morning sun. What vastness! Your skis stir impatiently. Is this descent 3 miles long? Four? More? You can tell from the tiny dots at the bottom—skiers!—that the distance is plenty enough to let you ski to your heart's content.

Suddenly, temptation gets the better of you, and you push yourself off in a flash of poles and shoot down the bowls.

Aspen, Colorado. It could also be Vail. Or Loveland Basin or Winter Park. Width and breadth are a western trademark.

Colorado! Skiing remains one of the state's major attractions: Colorado has more resorts and ski areas than most other states, east or west.

You tan easiest at these higher altitudes. You find fewer people on those giant mountains that streak up to 13,000 feet in the Rockies. You get more space for yourself, more lifts for your convenience, and a look at more advanced skiers whom you can copy. (The technical level is high.)

A skilled skier aims with precision; he or she can zip around a standing novice, can pick his or her way around trees, can jump a knoll without falling. If you become good at it, you can ski as fast or as slow as you please and still stop at a moment's notice. (That's the secret, of course—the ability to come to a halt.)

Let no one tell you differently: The snow is much, much better in Colorado's Rockies. It is light, fluffy, easy-to-ski snow, the kind that obeys you. (By contrast, eastern snow means a constant struggle: You must battle ice and more ice.) Eastern landscapes are pleasing to the eyes: gentle, wooded hills; white church spires;

rolling terrain. Colorado's western landscapes are grandiose. You feel a powerful impact when you look down into the valleys—far, far down—from the Crested Butte sundeck.

The state's ski meccas are justly famous.

None of Colorado's ski resorts look alike; each has its special character made up of a dozen variables. Century-old mining towns like Breckenridge and Crested Butte have been revived. Aspen is immense and complex. Vail is a giant in every way, an American St. Moritz. Winter Park serves vacationers during the week and young Denverites on weekends. Loveland Basin and Keystone yield good winter days, made up in unequal portions by sun-stroked faces, pure air, and a snowscape that tugs and pulls. Colorado's ski slopes seduce the passionate skier, give a great deal, but demand little in return. Only the correct motion and concentration.

If you come to this state anytime between late November and April, you should try to ski, even if you've never done it before.

For more information contact Colorado Ski Country USA, 1560 Broadway, Suite 1440, Denver 80202; (303) 837–0793.

PEACH HARVESTS

Noon at Palisade, Colorado. The golden peach of the sun has already climbed to the top of the trees, which stand out against a poster-blue sky. You've been in the ❖ **Clark Family Peach Orchards** since seven that morning, up and down the ladders. The guys in Denver's health clubs (pumping iron indoors) should envy you out there in the fresh country air. You've gulped big amounts of it, breathing deeply. No pollution. Your nostrils take in the Elberta peach bouquet.

You reach rhythmically for the warm, ripe fruit, which you plop into a sack hanging from your shoulders. When it's full, it weighs forty or fifty pounds, enough for the waiting baskets.

Your arms must stretch, your trunk must rotate, you keep bending. Your legs withstand the extra load; you rejoice in the climbing and descending from and to terra firma. In fact, you've gotten your second wind. Despite the heat, you accelerate before lunchtime. The bushels add up. The mood in the orchards is relaxed.

The pleasures of working a peach harvest shouldn't be underestimated. When other people must slave in office cubicles in dirty cities, some folks are outdoors, in the clean, sweet-smelling

57

orchards, getting paid for being in touch with trees and leaves and fruit. This is a pretty world for summer sport, with the colors lingering behind your eyelids for a long time.

At Palisade, on Colorado's Western Slope, you're into Elbertas. A collegian from Colorado Springs who has come to Palisade ever since he was a high schooler feels nostalgic about it. He says, "Peach time reminds me of homemade ice cream, or a secret treasure in the lunch box, a tantalizing centerpiece, or even a long drive back from the orchards amid bushels of tree-ripened Elbertas, munching on the way and saving the pits to plant."

Suddenly, it's late August, and the 310 growers in Palisade (which is 238 miles west of Denver) must round up some 4,000 harvesters to empty some 500,000 trees. The need can be so great at this juncture that the orchardists enlist the help of relatives, transients, hoboes (who arrive on freight trains), high school kids (nearby schools close for the occasion), laborers from Mexico, and university students, as well as yearly regulars headed by crew chiefs, who come to western Colorado for those two weeks.

In Colorado alone the bounty amounts to some 250,000 bushels. Because much of the harvesting is still done by hand, it takes an army of people to harvest, sort, and crate the peaches. This creates an incredible number of temporary jobs.

Negative aspects? Pay is minimal, by the bushel. Unless you're in good physical shape, you'll find it hard to scale ladders all day, to stretch your limbs until they ache. The string of your filled harvest sack bites without mercy into your shoulders or neck. You keep lugging forty-eight-pound bushels.

The work guarantees to make almost anyone lose weight. But you can't compare it to a tennis game in a breeze. In fact, some orchards—especially in those sun-baked, parched, wrinkled Colorado plateaus—get extremely hot. The canopy of trees is pierced by the sun's rays. Count on sweating a lot. You're only cool at 7:00 A.M. when you start, and in some parts of the country at 6:00 P.M. when you finish. (The Palisade Chamber of Commerce crows about the "354 days of sunshine.")

Some comers also forget about the peach fuzz. You won't feel it for a few hours, but after a day it stings. (Some persons are allergic to the fuzz and break out in hives.) Talcum can help the average harvester. But it remains a problem.

Benefits? You can easily make friends, learn about other harvests, get tips on where to split to next. In Palisade The Orchard Cafe is full of beer drinkers at night, hatching plots for the balance of the year and the coming seasons. Colorado peach harvesting is a trip that usually leads to another trip.

From Denver drive west on I–70 toward Grand Junction until you see the Palisade turnoff.

Do you sometimes think of visiting a turn-of-the-century fruit farm? The ◆ **Cross Orchards Living History Farm** in Grand Junction is a site listed on the National Register of Historic Places. And a tour of the facility—especially with children—can be memorable. Here are ancient tractors and other weather-beaten farm machinery, plus old tools. Here you can see the first gas pumps (offering gasoline at 14 cents a gallon). Costumed Cross Orchard staff members and volunteers demonstrate weaving, candle making, and blacksmithing circa 1896. A narrow-gauge railroad is still in place, and your kids are allowed to climb into the caboose.

The former Cross apple orchards can be visited from Memorial Day to Labor Day, sometimes even through October. The address is 3073 F Road, Grand Junction 81501; the phone is (303) 434–9814.

Tour de Moon is the name of the circular bike ride through the ◆ **Colorado National Monument.** This 37-mile loop on paved roads passes through stark and beautiful scenery. Pick up maps at the entrance station.

The Colorado National Monument is known for its steep plateaus, its sheer dropoffs, and its craggy rock spires.

From downtown Grand Junction follow Monument Road past the entry gate. From here the popular route is called Rim Rock Drive, and for good reason: The ascent to the top of the plateau is steep for a cyclist and requires good lungs and leg muscles.

But the views are worth it. From your open-air perch you'll absorb more of the Colorado scenery and atmosphere than those who pass you in automobiles. Remember that, in Colorado, state law says bicycles are considered vehicles and have to obey the same traffic laws as automobiles. Ride single-file on the right with traffic. Always signal when stopping or turning. When you need to catch your breath, move off the road. Use extra caution when passing through the short tunnels on this scenic ride.

Take a few minutes to stop at the Colorado Ute Monument Visitors Center before your final descent to the town of Fruita. From there Grand Junction is just a few miles away, along the Colorado River as you complete your tour loop.

NORTHWESTERN MOUNTAINS

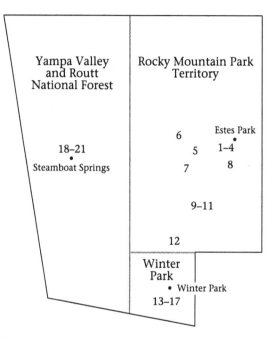

Yampa Valley
and Routt
National Forest

Rocky Mountain Park
Territory

18–21
•
Steamboat Springs

6
5
7

Estes Park
•
1–4

8

9–11

12

Winter
Park
• Winter Park

13–17

1. Stanley Hotel
2. Prospect Mountain
3. Trout Haven
4. Lake Estes
5. Ponderosa Lodge
6. Trail Ridge Road
7. Rocky Mountain
   National Park
8. Peaceful Valley Ranch
9. Grand Lake
10. Grand Lake Ski Touring
    Center
11. Riverside Guesthouses

12. C Lazy U Ranch
13. Winter Park
14. Beaver Village Condos
15. Hi Country Haus
16. Ski Idlewild
17. Junior Jumping School
18. Steamboat Springs Winter
    Carnival
19. Scandinavian Lodge
20. Jean-Paul Luc Winter Driving
    School
21. Vista Verde Guest & Ski
    Touring Ranch

Northwestern Mountains

Rocky Mountain Park Territory

If you happen to come to Estes Park at the high season—and want to be above the melee—you might consider the short uphill drive to the ❖ **Stanley Hotel.** It stands above the busy town like a white castle. The 100-room Stanley reminds you of those old Swiss Grand Hotels—aristocratic, flawlessly kept up, frequently restored, a monument to good taste and good manners. The hotel is all stately white columns, Victorian furniture, fireplaces crackling in the lobby, rooms with impeccable white linen, polished cherrywood furniture, and antique dressers. The handwrought leaded-glass windows, the spotless white tablecloths in the (deluxe) dining room, and the comfortable bar add to a vacation feeling. Miles of walks surround the hostelry, which is at an elevation of 7,500 feet.

The historic hotel was built by the inventor of the Stanley Steamer automobile. Back in 1905 doctors gave F. O. Stanley, the inventor, only a few months to live. Stanley gathered his wife, her maid, and his controversial Steamer and headed for the Colorado Rockies. The undaunted old gentleman was determined to drive his vehicle to Estes Park, Colorado, regardless of roads declared impassable. He victoriously covered the 20-mile stretch in a record one hour and fifty minutes. The inventor suffered from tuberculosis, and his doctor had sent him to Estes Park with the hope of prolonging the patient's life "for a year or so." The sturdy old gentleman was to live for another thirty-seven years. (He reached the age of ninety-one.)

The ingenious, eccentric millionaire ran his lavish hotel facility with a style all his own. In order to bring chamber music to Estes Park for his guests, he had a huge New York Steinway piano shipped to Colorado by ox cart. His resort, located on 160 acres of land, was part of the 6,000-acre Lord Dunraven hunting estate.

Most of the guests arrived by train, to be picked up in Stanley's steaming ten-horsepower automobile. The "all-electric" hotel charged $8.00 a day, gourmet meals included.

The Stanley Hotel opened in June 1910. It had cost $1 million to build and was described as "simply palatial." The materials had come by horse teams on roads that Stanley himself designed. A magnificent white edifice with dormers and flagpoles and elegant porches welcomed the hotel guests. Once inside the lobby, the arrivals were dazzled by the hand-carved wooden staircase, the ornate brass elevator, and the carpeted halls that led to rooms with leaded-glass windows and four-poster beds.

Stanley, who'd made huge sums with the invention of his automobile and later with photo-dry plates, personally designed the hotel's electric kitchens. He ordered the decor of a music room, arranged for a gentlemen's smoking room (even if he never touched tobacco himself), and enjoyed showing up in the billiard room. The legendary Stanley Hotel eventually attracted celebrities such as Theodore Roosevelt, John Philip Sousa, and Molly Brown.

Remarkably enough, F. O. Stanley's creation still stands; indeed, it prospers. It can be found in the National Register of Historic Places. The music room is still there, as is a writing room. Picture windows and restaurant views give to the mountains, including Longs Peak. Sunning and swimming are available in summer. An outstanding theater flourishes; in fact, the hotel stays open through the winters as well. Rates are moderate when the snow falls; summer accommodations are expensive, as they should be at this palace.

A 1906 Stanley Steamer automobile stands in the lobby, as a reminder of how it all began.

Stanley Hotel, P.O. Box 1767, Estes Park 80517; (303) 586–3371. In Colorado: (800) ROCKIES.

On a July day in 1982, a flood roared into one of Colorado's most visited tourists centers. The water raged through Elkhorn Avenue, Estes Park's main street, breaking shop windows, causing wholesale destruction. The Fall River rose, tearing into motels and mountain cabins. Three drowned. The damage was estimated at $31 million. Worse, that season—and part of the next—the flood stopped tourism in its tracks.

Estes Park has long been rebuilt. The reborn main street offers prettily painted benches, trees and planters, new sidewalks, and souvenir stores. A church has become an array of shops. Someone coined the slogan "The Gutsiest Little Town in Colorado!" Some 250,000 tourists come to stay here each year. They enjoy themselves in a myriad of ways. They flock to the nearby Rocky Mountain

63

National Park. They scale the Twin Owl rocks; you can see the climbers in town, hung with hardware, ropes slung across their chests. Other visitors carry fishing tackle; trout are plentiful (Colorado license required). Wildlife abounds, and the air is pure in the surrounding mountains.

Estes Park has two golf courses, including one that occupies land once owned by the famous Earl of Dunraven, an Irish nobleman who discovered the area in 1827 while on a hunting trip. The American homesteaders followed during the 1870s. Nowadays Estes Park has about 7,000 permanent inhabitants, plus 25,000 others who own mountain cabins and show up briefly in summer and often keep to themselves.

To be sure, the town is ideal for vacationing families. Estes makes boredom an impossibility. In summer an aerial tram rises to ◆ **Prospect Mountain,** a few blocks from Elkhorn Avenue. ◆**Trout Haven,** also close by, features several ponds stocked with rainbows, plus gear for rent. On nearby ◆ **Lake Estes** you discover boating possibilities. Access to family hiking terrain is free and almost unlimited. For those who prefer to do their nature exploration by automobile, a drive along the spectacular 50-mile-long Trail Ridge Road in the Rocky Mountain National Park is recommended.

The reborn Estes Park presents some contrasts: new and old, serene and loud, natural and artificial. The touristy aspects of the town will disturb the sensitive traveler. Mountains don't seem to suffice. Your children can race noisy little go-carts ("Grand Prix! Thrilling! A Blast!"). On Elkhorn Avenue a store prints handbills with headlines ("The Smiths Having a Ball in Estes!" or "Patsy Saw Her First Snow!!") or sells T-shirts with silly messages ("Colorado is owned by Canadians").

For all visitors there are rodeos, parades, chamber music concerts, Rocky Mountain National Park talks, walks, and campfire programs. Still other possibilities: You can shop for Native American crafts or jewelry, for sporting goods, western wear, or mineral specimens.

When should you come to Estes Park? Avoid July and August: Elkhorn Avenue then turns into a tourism circus, with thousands of people descending upon the town. Early June and September are good months. A tranquil time begins after Labor Day.

Accommodations? The redecorated ◆**Ponderosa Lodge** overlooks the now peaceful Fall River; some units were damaged by the flood but rebuilt (Fall River Road, Highway 34, Estes Park 80517; 303–586–4233). The YMCA in the Rockies rents housekeeping cabins. Estes Park has a Holiday Inn with a large indoor swimming pool. The Stanley Hotel is the most elegant and historic in town. Except for the moderately priced YMCA, the tariff for *summer* accommodations is expensive.

The trip to Estes is worth your while. The flood is past history now, water under the bridge. The "Gutsiest Little Town in Colorado" thrives again.

Estes Park is 65 miles northwest of Denver and easy to reach via the Boulder Turnpike and US36 through Lyons. For more information, write Estes Park Chamber of Commerce, Estes Park 80517; (800) 44–ESTES.

Superlatives? Consider ◆**Trail Ridge Road** in the 415-square-mile Rocky Mountain National Park, connecting the towns of Grand Lake and Estes Park. The road is the highest continuously paved highway in the United States. More? It's one of the highest such connections for automobiles; it allows you to drive for 11 miles above the 11,000-foot level, above timberline, face to face with mountain giants that rival those of Switzerland.

The season is short for a visit, though. Deep snows and snow drifts cover Trail Ridge all winter; indeed, the famous road is open only from Memorial Day until the first heavy snowfall, usually in mid-October. Then it closes down. Grand Lake and Estes Park are 50 road miles apart.

Dazzling figures: You climb for 4,700 feet on a highway that has serpentines like those of Alpine passes. At one point you reach the 12,183-foot (3,713-meter) level, where the air is thin and the ultraviolet rays are strong; then you descend to Grand Lake, which is 4,000 feet below. In between you spot some of Colorado's highest mountain ranges; when you park, you find yourself in view of rock piles deposited here during the Ice Age, known as moraines. There's the Iceberg Lake View at 12,080 feet, and there's a high meadowland known as Tundra, which is reminiscent of Alaska.

Your family can learn much about forestry below timberline: The lovely aspen tree occurs in stands at elevations of about 9,000 to 10,000 feet. Trail Ridge Road also provides a home for alder trees and Douglas fir. In the conifer family you find blue spruce, lodgepole pines, and the beautiful *Pinus ponderosa*. At

65

some higher levels, 9,500 feet and up, grow the subalpine fir, lodgepole pine, and the Engelmann spruce.

How do you distinguish between the many species of conifers? The differences are noticeable. Spruces, for example, can be identified by cones that stand up straight like candles, and spruce needles are attached singly to the twigs. By contrast, ponderosa pine needles come in clusters of two to three; the bark is a dark brown. Lodgepole pine needles are attached in pairs.

Like most important Colorado highways, Trail Ridge has a long history. First came the Utes and other Native American tribes, who actually followed the already marked trails of wild animals. Miners used it in the 1880s. In 1929 Congress appropriated almost $500,000—a large sum in those days—to build a highway over the Continental Divide. Engineers called it Tombstone Ridge, which became Trail Ridge Road. The paving was finally completed in 1935. The government engineers, normally cool and scientific, became eloquent enough in their final analysis, which mentioned the "deep canyons, many lakes and perpetual snow." The route report concluded: "Below lie streams, valleys, forested slopes, and the realms of civilization. All around are mountains and peaks, no longer towering above but close at hand or seen across some mighty valley."

Travel some 70 miles north and west from Denver (I–25 north to SR66, west on 66 until it joins US36) to Estes Park and Trail Ridge Road.

One hundred years ago, an Englishwoman named Isabella Bird waxed enthusiastic about Colorado's landscape. She came upon the Longs Peak region on horseback. What expressions of wonder! "Exquisite stretches of flowery pastures dotted with trees sloping down-like to bright streams full of red waistcoated trout or running up in soft glades into the dark forest, above which the snow peaks rise," wrote the lady, and the description still fits.

The peaks and lakes at ◆ **Rocky Mountain National Park** have present-day names that bear witness to it all: The tourist can view Deer Mountain, Isolation Peak, Snowdrift Peak. Those who come afoot—and more people do every year—may head for Dream Lake, Lone Pine Lake, Fern Lake, and up to Chasm Lake.

All belong to the stunning 415-square-mile span of the Rocky Mountain National Park. Established by the federal government in 1915, the park now encompasses more than one hundred upthrusting peaks above 11,000 feet above sea level. Longs Peak is the highest mountain in the park at 14,255 feet.

The park's assets exceed those of many other national parks. There are more things to do here, yet the expanse also brings happiness to the inactive. Nearby resort hotels are inviting with clean rooms and deck chairs, and the park appeals to the most sedentary motorist.

Nature studies, lectures, and tours are conducted by park rangers. The park's many summer doings make the area especially attractive to tourists. There are not only campfire programs but also a number of short self-guiding nature paths for the benefit of families. (You can bring small children, too.) A Colorado fishing license entitles you to angle for trout in the park's many lakes; some 350 well-marked trails invite the hiker. Wildflowers abound in late spring.

Walking is the best way to see this national park. One of the most scenic and easily accessed trails is the one to Bear Lake. Nine different hikes begin here. Difficulty ratings range from the $\frac{1}{2}$-mile "easy" stroll around the lake to the $8\frac{8}{10}$-mile round-trip to Flattop Mountain. This is rated "strenuous." Rocky Mountain National Park is especially popular with backpackers, who need a permit, and with rock climbers. The most difficult climb is Longs Peak Diamond, fit only for elite Alpinists.

The Park Service exacts a small fee to enter the mountainous domain; if you plan to visit other parks, it will be worth your while to buy a Golden Eagle Passport. It's good for your car and its occupants during the entire year. Travelers aged sixty-two years and over may ask for a Golden Age permit. Hikers can reach the park gratis by setting out from the main parking lot of the Longs Peak Trail toward Chasm Lake, below the summit of the peak. The trails are marked and not too steep.

Please note that the Rocky Mountain National Park has become so popular that every year nearly 2½ million people stream through each of the three entrances, especially in summer. The major highway, Trail Ridge Road, closes mid-October through Memorial Day.

Rocky Mountain has only five campgrounds, which is less than a third of Yosemite's or Yellowstone's. No hookups are available for trailers; the big ones, like Airstreams, are hard to navigate in the park. Some tents already go up early in the morning, and at the peak of the season—June through Labor Day—accommodations may be hard to come by even in neighboring towns.

67

There are several ways to avoid the crowds and still enjoy the Rockies' pleasantly cool summers; the green of pine, spruce, and fir; the mosaic of wildflowers; and the water that cascades down those Rockies. For instance, you can arrive early in the seasons or after the children are back in school. You can relax by renting a mountain cabin.

Autumn is the best time of all. Coloradans call it Indian Summer; it means a seemingly endless string of clear, warm days. The evenings turn crisp and the nights are chilly, so bring an overcoat. Mid-September seems the best period. Come after Labor Day, and you'll find less competition for the area's good rooms, restaurant tables, and traffic lanes.

In winter cross-country skiing is plentiful. In summer the patient animal watcher can see deer, elk, sheep, beaver, pikas, and many birds as well.

The Englishwoman was right about the park and its "exquisite stretches."

From Denver you can reach this ultrascenic region via several routes. Some summer motorists head west from the Mile High City on I-70, cross Berthoud Pass via US40, and then arrive in the Rocky Mountain National Park via Grand Lake (altitude 8,367 feet and icicle-cold). You can also come on the spectacular Peak to Peak Highway (SR119, SR72, and SR7) from Black Hawk. The drive is especially enjoyable in late fall when the aspen trees burst into gold. Earmark at least half a day to get to the national park via this route. To save time you can drive through Boulder and Lyons instead (use US36); from Boulder it's about 34 miles to Estes Park and the Rocky Mountain National Park gates.

Here's Colorado's only lodge and guest ranch that has its own little mountaintop chapel—an Austrian one with an onion steeple and a big European bell that sounds meal hours. A brass plaque on the outside of the always open chapel tells us about the dedication and reminds us "to open the eyes and hearts to the beauty and mightiness of His Creation—to all who worship here, may the chapel instill awareness of His Omnipresence."

The ◆**Peaceful Valley Ranch** is located above Lyons; you get there from Denver via the dramatic Middle St. Vrain SR7 and SR72. Moderate rates include family-style meals. Call (303) 747-2881.

In August every year ◆**Grand Lake**—the largest glacial lake

68

in the state—is dotted with sailboats. The marinas fill up with yachtsmen and -women. The mountain giants of Rocky Mountain National Park lord over the stunning scene. The lake waters are unusually blue. At an elevation of almost 8,400 feet above sea level, Grand Lake—lake and community—boasts "the World's Highest Yacht Club." And best of all, Grand Lake is somewhat off the beaten path. You can't get there directly by the famous 13-mile long Trail Ridge Road. And US40 to Denver doesn't connect with Grand Lake, either; you need to come via US34.

The slightly offbeat location doesn't prevent the international sailing elite from competing here for trophies. Regattas are frequent. The marinas get busy with summer tourists who rent rowboats, paddleboats, or motorboats. You see sailboarders. The lake and the nearby streams are populated by anglers. Four river-rafting companies take you out on various excursions. You have limitless opportunities for hiking. Stables beckon with horses. The surrounding peaks are forested by healthy aspen trees, ponderosa pine, and Douglas fir. You will find waterfalls and mountain flowers.

In winter the little western town shuts down somewhat; the handsome wooden lakeshore summer homes are abandoned by their rich midwestern and Texas owners; the souvenir shops along the boardwalk close down. Only a few saloons, a tiny grocery, and the pharmacy stay open. Trail Ridge Road is closed. At the same time, the cross-country ski possibilities are plentiful; the Rocky Mountain National Park entrance is only a mile away, and you see skiers even on the golf course. Noisy snowmobile enthusiasts show up with their machines. Most winter tourists stay in nearby Granby; the wealthy ones repair to the C Lazy U Ranch.

For those who wish to enjoy the deep silence that winter in the Rockies can bring, the smell and roar of snowmobiles shatters any attempt to enjoy the deep quiet of winter.

One escape from the snowmobiles: the ◆ **Grand Lake Ski Touring Center** (Box 590, Grand Lake 80447). Although few people know about it, the location is easy to find; just turn left on County Road 48 and proceed to the west entrance of Rocky Mountain National Park. The Ski Touring Center is more scenic than most, and the 16 miles (25 kilometers) of trails are immaculately kept. Some of the runs are surprisingly steep—especially for a golf course!—but other trails are gentle enough for beginners. Among the many runs, experts will enjoy the "Spirits

Haunt"; good skiers can be seen on "Ptarmigan Tuck." Actually, you rarely see many people up here in this pristine territory; Grand Lake just doesn't get many visitors in winter. And, of course, snowmobiles are verboten in the Ski Touring Center. For more information: (303) 627–8008.

Grand Lake has lots of summer cabins for rent. Some of the most appealing lodgings are in a series of log cabins known as the ◆ **Riverside Guesthouses** (phone: 303–627–3619). The owners gave nature names to units, like Juniper, Tumbleweed, Alder, or Chickadee. In the area, housekeeping rooms and some motels are available, too. The cool air of these elevations appeals to southerners. Rates during the summer season range from moderate to high.

Grand Lake's history is also worth writing about. The Native Americans called it Spirit Lake. According to local historians, the first Indians arrived around A.D. 900 to 1300. They no doubt stayed during the summer and late fall. Game, fish, and other food were plentiful.

The earliest legend of the region tells of Ute, Arapaho and Cheyenne squabbles. Apparently, the Utes living in this summer paradise were suddenly attacked by marauding Cheyennes. Fearing for their women and children, the Ute braves hastily loaded them on rafts and shoved the rafts onto the lake for safety. As the battle with the Cheyennes raged among the trees and along the lakeshore, a storm came up, blowing the rafts far out onto the 400-foot-deep lake. The Indians watched helplessly as the rafts were overturned and the women and children drowned. After this time the Utes regarded the lake as dangerous and stayed away, naming it Spirit Lake.

The first white visitors probably showed up in 1855 to hunt for furs and catch the plentiful trout. Although he is best known for his discovery of the Gore Range near Vail, Sir George Gore, the Irish nobleman, also explored the Grand Lake wilderness for a couple of years. He arrived with a party of fifty persons and thirty supply wagons. He brought guides, secretaries, and hunt-and-fish-supply artisans. The country then abounded with game, including elk, bear, deer, and buffalo.

Other hunters and trappers of lesser stature came next, and some, attracted by the remote beauty of the area, remained to become the region's first settlers. Among these was Joseph L.

Westcott, who became the first postmaster of Grand Lake in 1877. Westcott, later known as Judge Westcott, remained here most of his life.

In 1881 the little hamlet of Grand Lake got its first sizable general store, and the Grand Central Hotel was completed. It was a decade of summer residents building homes that looked out on the water. The first big regatta took place here in 1912, on the 12-mile-long lake. It is measured only a mile across, so you always see the other shore. The mountain backdrop is as stunning as any in Switzerland.

Take I–70 from Denver until you see the exit to US40; follow it to Granby, where you reach Grand Lake via US34. For more information: Grand Lake Area Chamber of Commerce, P.O. Box 57, Grand Lake 80477; (303) 627–3402.

The ◆ C Lazy U Ranch, ensconced in its own Willow Creek Valley some 100 miles west of Denver, is no ordinary guest ranch.

At the stables the wranglers assign you a personal horse for your stay, and you and your group set out into a quiet, slightly remote, truly relaxing 5,000 acres of mountains and hillsides, forests and rivers, ponds and lookout points.

In winter the ranch turns into Grandma Moses scenery, all white, with brown barns and fences and the children—colored dots—playing ice hockey, skating, and tubing. At the Nordic shop one hundred pairs of cross-country skis and boots and poles await the lucky guests. Some 30 miles of trails are packed and ready; you share these winter woods with elk and deer, which show up in the meadows, stealing the horses' hay. You ski in privacy, in a private preserve. When the snow falls, the summer's wranglers turn into cross-country guides. No extra charge for lessons or rentals.

Rates are high and commensurate with the ranch's amenities. C Lazy U is closed in October and November and in April and May. Access: I–70 to exit 232, then along US40 to SR125. You'll see the sign. For more information: C Lazy U Ranch, P.O. Box 378A, Granby 80446; (303) 887–3344.

WINTER PARK

How does a large ski area come to be? Where did it all start? To understand ◆ Winter Park and its landscape better, some historical background may be in order.

A few hardy Denverites already skied in the region around 1920. Winter Park (then West Portal) consisted of sawmills and railroad shanties; a tunnel construction shack served as a warming house to skiers who sought their thrills in forest glades and down logging roads. They climbed the Winter Park hills under their own steam, all the while dreaming of real trails. The dream became a reality in the mid-1930s when several ski clubs laid out better runs.

Denver's manager of parks and improvements was among the first to see the potential. He appropriated the funds for a first ski tow, a T-bar of sorts, built with staves from old whiskey barrels. In March 1937 the Denver official told an astonished Colorado audience "We'll create a winter playground unequaled in the world!" He brought in Otto Schniebs, then one of America's most famous skiers. Schniebs, who spoke of the sport as "a way of life," was enthusiastic about the runs.

Winter Park's official dedication took place on January 28, 1940. A ski band played. Hans Hauser, a handsome ski school director, had been commandeered from Austria. Alf Engen, the jumper, came from Utah to show his stuff. A ticket for the ½-mile-long lift cost $1.00 (50 cents for students).

By 1947 Winter Park (which got its name from its designation as a winter park in Denver's park system) had three T-bar lifts and four rope tows. Owned by the city of Denver, the area made good progress during the early fifties; soon there were numerous chairlifts, which multiplied every season. (The area now has nineteen lifts.)

The history of this ski mecca was crowned in 1975 when its capacity was almost doubled. To drum up $6 million for lift construction and base facilities seems an even greater feat when you consider the tight money situation of the early seventies.

Twin factors—fairly easy access and adequate accommodations—always helped Winter Park's cause. A Ski Weeker requires no car at this destination resort. To cut costs many families come directly from Denver International Airport (DIA) via a special daily express bus.

To be sure, Winter Park always attracted Ski Week customers of every age and ability. The slopes are well groomed. The lifts run without fail. A large ski school teaches beginners in record time; three days of lessons should get you up and down most slopes.

The area boasts more than a hundred ski runs that satisfy the most fanatic racer and the rank novice.

Winter Park vies with Colorado's top resorts, yet it has none of the poshness, the celebrity parade, the hectic atmosphere of other international ski resorts, the wild night life of the Beautiful People. The resort works out well for nonskiers also. Winter Park's managers make it possible for anyone to reach the Mary Jane summit (elevation 12,025 feet) in comfortable, heated vehicles called Sprites. For a few dollars a vacationer can thus mingle with the fast downhill crowd, take pictures of the deep sun-flecked woods, and lunch al fresco. Several ski lodges offer heated swimming pools, and even older persons like to spend a few unstrenuous hours on light cross-country skis.

Sleigh rides are available in the evenings. The families climb aboard, snuggle under warm blankets, breathe the forest air, and listen to the sleigh bells and the crunch of snow. Along the way, there will be hot chocolate for the kids, hot spiced wine for adults. In the same Colorado valley, at the same time, vacationers enjoy themselves on a lighted hill, slithering down the slopes on snow tubes.

The 67-mile drive across Berthoud Pass to Winter Park won't take much longer than two hours on I–70 and US40. The roads are kept sanded.

Reveille to a winter morning in the Colorado Ski Country. Outside your windows, the sun slants through the conifers; from the condo cross-country ski tracks take off for the snow-covered forest. You're on the quiet edge of the town of Winter Park. You gratefully set out, skiing through light and shade, breathing deeply. Ah, to be alive! To be in motion!

Later you return to the comfortable condominium for lunch. Some people are unaware that they can rent these vacation apartments for a night or a weekend, solo, coupled, or as a family of six. Kristine Meyer, one of the managers at the ◆**Beaver Village Condos,** puts it this way: "Your time with us will be special. You can cross-country ski outside your door or catch a free shuttle to Winter Park's downhill runs. Afterward, you can sit in our sauna, enjoy a whirlpool, or swim in the indoor pool. It's all included."

Beaver Village is typical for Colorado's condo goodies: a well-equipped kitchen, matching dishes, pots and pans, ironed sheets, clean towels, shiny glassware, cozy, generous furniture in earth colors. The 165 units contain moss-covered fireplaces, plus wood.

73

And each *room* has its own thermostat. The management hands honeymooners a gratis bottle of vintage wine. The Beaver Village Condominiums are managed by Nick Teverbuagh. Reservations at P.O. Box 349, Winter Park 84082; (303) 726–8813 or (800) 824–8438.

At the west end of town, the somewhat larger ◆ **Hi Country Haus** complex is tucked away among the trees on both sides of the Fraser River. This is more than a house, of course, but a 306-condo resort in its own right, complete with recreation center, a glass palace full of hot tubs, a grocery store, buses to take you to the Winter Park and Mary Jane lifts, and even private cross-country trails that connect with Idlewild's touring terrain.

The Hi Country Haus condos run true to form: fine kitchen cabinetry, microwave ovens, dishwashers, beamed living-room ceilings. Dave Smith, one of the longtime executives, uses the slogan, "We're a home away from home." Most of the staff, including president Mike Dybicz, have been here for many years; they know how to run a vacation community.

This is Winter Park's oldest and largest condo complex, and Hi Country Haus service is rapid. Example? You can't seem to get a certain channel on your television set. You call the office; almost at once the television repairman shows up to fix the problem. Size doesn't mean impersonality here; some of the units certainly reflect the owners. In unit 1501, for instance, the coffee mugs come with personal greetings:

> *My best to you*
> *Each Day*
> *My best for you*
> *Each Day*

For reservations: Hi Country Haus Condominiums, Box 3095, Winter Park 80482; (303) 825–0705 or (800) 228–1025. The setup is ideal for groups, and Dave Smith gets lots of them. Actually, Smith's outfit correctly bears the name Winter Park Vacations, which offers six other properties, all managed by the same company and accessed via the above phone and address.

Several times each winter the slopes of this giant area are alive with multicolored pairs of flags, and through these gates, at intervals, there descend a succession of skiers. In a downhill race they're clocked at 40 miles an hour.

Nothing unusual? Not for the ordinary ski racer. But these people are not ordinary. Many of the competitors have only one leg. Others have only one arm or no hands. The rest fly down the Colorado mountain despite paralyzed joints, missing kneecaps, absent toes, or stiffened backs.

The skiers are all physically challenged, the result of disease, accidents, or their conditions at birth. Yet these people show that you can conquer almost any barrier. Eyes shining, cheeks glowing, the racers speed through the finish line.

Colorado's Winter Park Ski Resort offers the world's largest teaching program for physically challenged skiers. Some thousand volunteer and fifteen professional instructors participate in it. Each ski season thousands of lessons are given here to people with cerebral palsy, spina bifida, polio, multiple sclerosis, and paraplegia. Some of the students are blind. All in all, forty-five different disabilities are handled in Winter Park.

Skiing requires perfect coordination and a good balance. To hurtle down a snowy slope, a two-legged sighted skier uses all his God-given limbs—his feet to direct the two skis, his hands and arms to hold the poles, which act as stabilizers.

The loss of an arm throws the body out of kilter. With only one ski pole, it's more difficult to make the turns or to walk up a hill. Yet where there's a will, there's a way, and practice and determination will make a one-armed skier as good as a two-armed one.

The sudden loss of a leg is more serious, yet even that can be overcome. At first there will be pain, and when the stump has healed, the person will feel off-balance. Then come the weeks of learning the use of crutches. The amputee must strengthen the remaining leg—and how the muscles will ache for a while! There's also the self-consciousness. But only at first.

A positive mental attitude will put the physically challenged person onto the right track within a few weeks. The individual realizes that one can do many things with an incomplete body. Winter Park simply calls it "rehabilitation through recreation." The students themselves often see it as a lark. "Skiing on one leg is easier than on two," chuckles one participant. "The trouble with *two* skis is that they don't go in the same direction for the beginner!"

A Member of the Colorado Handicap Program

The Colorado Handicap Program started in 1970 and has become the largest of its kind in the world. The program began with twenty-three amputees from Denver's Children's Hospital, and each year new disabilities were added. Most of the students are now adults. One of the highlights has been the introduction of the Arroya, a sledlike device used by paraplegics or any individual confined to a wheelchair.

Skiers with one good leg and two usable arms are taught the three-tracking technique, which means skiing with small outriggers. The outriggers consist of a ski tip attached to the bottom of a modified crutch. In full gear, the three-tracker has contact with the snow on the bottom of the full-length ski and balances with both ski tips. In due time amputee skiers become so proficient that they can enter races.

How it is possible to teach skiing to the sightless? In some countries instructors ring a little bell at every dip of a mountain. Winter Park has used bamboo poles that link instructor and pupil; the key teaching elements, however, are touch and verbal contact. The sightless individual has to begin from the beginning: He or she has to learn all about ski boots (and how to put them on) and then about the skis themselves. The feeling of standing on skis comes next, with the feet parallel to each other, then walking to the sound of the instructor's ski poles tapping.

Next the pupil sidesteps up a gentle slope, constantly in communication with the instructor. Chairlift loading has to be taught, too. Again, with proper instruction and good communication, it proves to be no problem.

The sightless person eventually moves on to steered turns, parallel turns, and, finally, mogul skiing. Oftentimes a sightless skier will progress down the hill to the sound of the instructor calling, "Turn, turn, turn!" In due time a close bond develops between student and instructor.

How is this large Colorado program financed? Funds come from general donations, program fees, grants from private corporations and foundations, and special events. A large Denver bank finances a major race. The participants also pay a small daily fee toward lessons and equipment rental.

The learning experience isn't too difficult for athletic individuals who already skied before injury or illness hit them. Thanks to the use of special gear, people can now take up skiing despite physical problems.

One good example is Larry Kunz, who was born with a spina bifida condition that gave him little muscle control from the knees down. Thanks to Denver's Children's Hospital, Larry was introduced to Hal O'Leary, the Winter Park coach who specializes in teaching the physically impaired. "At first Larry couldn't even walk," O'Leary says. "But in a week, he was able to use his crutch skis and get around in heavy ski boots. Today, he soars down the slopes despite his spina bifida."

Some of the most exciting moments occur on the race course. At one competition a Winter Park official handed out trophies to the three fastest skiers. "You three won this slalom," he said. "But actually, all you people were winners. You won over your disability."

More information on the program can be obtained by writing or calling National Sports Center for the Disabled, P.O. Box 36, Winter Park 80482; (800) 453–2525.

Honestly now, did you ever dream of a family ski vacation yet not dared to go because the resorts all seemed too big, too famous, too overrun, or too expensive?

Hesitate no longer. Small can be beautiful, too. And to the novice skier, less can indeed be more.

A case in point? ◆ **Ski Idlewild,** a miniresort 3 miles west of Winter Park, has an excellent cross-country program. It aims almost exclusively at those who have never stood on the thin, wooden Nordic cross-country skis before. You learn to use them within a few hours. Your guide takes you up into Idlewild's conifer forests. The landscape here is kindly, too. And your guide-teacher will often stop to point out the tracks of deer, ermine, or snowshoe rabbits. The trails reflect the character of this country. You tour along a "Winterwoods" trail and descend a "Serendipity" path. Cross-country headquarters are situated in an old red barn. The barn stands amid lovely white meadows flanked by frozen ponds and a little river. The scenery is relaxing. Someone actually suggested that Idlewild change its name to "Idyllwild." Perhaps so; you're off the highway, away from the thunder of trucks and the caravan of cars. You can park yours here and forget it.

The Ski Idlewild setup includes accommodations at the nearby Hi Country Haus condos. After supper enjoy the sleigh rides, excursions to a nearby lighted tubing hill. It's all fairly low-key and informal. Ski Idlewild is 69 miles west of Denver via I–70 and US40. The phone number is (303) 726–5564.

High up, the ski jumper pushes off, sinks into a crouch, chest tight against his knees. He accelerates in the two steep snow grooves toward the platform. Suddenly, his body uncoils, straightens, dives upward. He is airborne. Seconds tick away. The spectators gasp. Still he soars through the Colorado sky, then a smooth landing. Judges note the distance. The audience roars.

Ski jumping is sensational to watch. Especially in this case.

The competitor was six years old! And his leap was the result of a unique school for youngsters at Winter Park. For the past several decades, thousands of kids have been trained here at ◆**Junior Jumping School** in human aviation. Children begin training at the age of six. The upper limit for competitors is eighteen. Even middle-aged parents have turned up for lessons. And why not? The school is for first-timers. There is a small charge to enroll on a regular basis. Anyone from any state is welcome to take advantage of it. Come to this Christmas-tree country any Saturday and Sunday during the entire ski season for all or parts of the program. You can talk to the instructors.

The Winter Park Recreational Association, which runs the popular Winter Park ski area, foots most of the bill for this sport. All jumping coaches are adults.

During the season's first get-together, anxious parents ask: Could a child come to harm here? Ski jumping is actually much safer than downhill skiing. For one thing, the special hills are well prepared. For another, you jump in a straight line, and training is worked out with great care. No person therefore ever suffered a serious accident at this Colorado school.

Before being taken on, a youngster must know how to ski at least a little. The instructor gives a brief test for this purpose. Then he groups his pupils by age. Class I is for sixteen- to eighteen-year-olds; Class II includes ages fourteen and fifteen; Class III, twelve and thirteen; Class IV, the nine- to eleven-year-olds; and Class V, under nine. All are taught separately. Fortunately, Winter Park's Junior Jumping School is lighthearted enough for an occasional snowball fight, and there are neither roll calls nor other regimentation.

How do you create a young ski jumper? The novices first learn the basic aerodynamic position for the inrun, meaning the short chute spurt before takeoff. They're taught the precise instant for leaping. They're shown how to stop safely and gracefully. In between are various exercises. When the youngsters are ready to make actual jumps, they always start with the smallest hills.

You only fly for a few feet here, but you get an idea of what it's like. A few tyros may at first have their hearts in their throats. After a single leap, though, the kids like the flight so much that they come back for more. Dropouts are rare. Most of the little jumpers feel like conquerors. "I'm a pilot!" they cry. "I'm a bird!" "Look at me! I'm a kite!"

A few jumps later you graduate to bigger hills, where you can zoom 30, 40, or more feet. In all, Winter Park has seven jumping installations. The largest, which is only for teenagers, allows distances of 200 feet; here speeds of 55 miles per hour are normal. In addition to coaching, Winter Park arranges for at least six competitions on every jumping hill. And from time to time, the winners battle it out at other Colorado ski areas as well. To be sent to Steamboat Springs or Summit County is a great honor, of course.

The jumping meets pack the greatest excitement, both for the young athletes and for the spectators. The eager freckled faces, the colorful sweaters, the splashes of reds, greens, and blues of parkas and ski pants and caps are a delightful sight. Before each leap tension fills the thin, sweet mountain air. Up on top the eyes squint under big goggles. Competitors get last-minute advice from instructors. Five-year-olds wonder: Will they jump far enough? Will they look good enough in the air? Will they beat the competition?

These junior affairs are staged much like adult championships: The entrants wear bibs with starting numbers. The reporters are there; the ski patrol stands by in case of the rare sprain; the judges sit sternly in a tower, ready to compute results. The jumpers are judged not only by what distances they can reach but also by their style. They lose points, for instance, by standing straight after takeoff. (The jumper must be forward while in flight.) They lose points if their skis flutter in all directions. (The skis must be together.) They cannot win if their arms go like windmills. And they're evaluated for their landing—which should be steady—and for the ease of coming to a halt (no hands).

This is the real thing, and even the tiniest of the fifty to seventy-five youngsters try to do their best. Afterward the kids get ribbons, and the year's final championship means a trophy for at least one jumper. Fortunately, even the losers receive a prize; it's a school shoulder patch for their parkas. You'll see moppets wearing this insignia with great pride.

Some of the jumpers keep training until the sun goes down behind the darkened fir trees. The youngsters struggle upward to fling themselves into the sky, soaring and soaring. At a time when we're often told that the American youth is going soft, Winter Park must command attention. Soft? The fresh, scrubbed, entrancing faces may look it. But after one or two winters, these leaping children become as hard as the steel edges under their skis. Surely, some of them will do us proud in a future Olympics!

Winter Park Competition Center, P.O. Box 36, Winter Park 80482; (303) 726–5514.

YAMPA VALLEY AND ROUTT NATIONAL FOREST

In 1875 James Crawford, the first white settler of Steamboat Springs, arrived here from Missouri with two wagons, his family, his horses, and a few head of cattle. He was attracted to the area by a newspaper article. The author of the piece described his view from the top of the Park Mountain Range as "a wilderness of mountain peaks and beautiful valleys, dark forests and silvery streams—a deserted land except for immense herds of elk and deer and buffalo which had not yet learned by experience to shun the presence of man."

The Yampa Valley's idyllic setting and mild climate made the eventual "presence of man" inevitable. Even before Crawford built his log cabin along the west bank of Soda Creek, the Yampa Valley had sheltered Ute Indians and, later, French and English fur trappers. (Legend has it that French fur trappers named the town Steamboat Springs because of the peculiar chugging sound from the hot springs near the river.)

Cattle ranchers had found Steamboat's emerald-green slopes ideal for fattening their herds en route to market. Hot and cold running water in the forms of three creeks, numerous hot springs, and the flow of the Yampa River lured more and more settlers to the valley.

Recreational skiing first came to Steamboat in the early 1900s when Norwegian Carl Howelson introduced the sports of ski jumping and ski racing to the community.

81

They've skied in "Ski Town U.S.A." facing Main Street before the turn of the century on long boards, with a long staff, the women in long skirts. They've jumped here from a giant hill before many other people thought of such things. For years, they've taught Steamboat youngsters to ski, gratis, from kindergarten up, all through high school, and through the small local college. Men with first names like Alf, Ansten, Lars, and Ragnar showed off their telemark turns way back when, and Steamboat Springs skiers—immigrants as well as natives—showed the world what they were made of. Many Olympians cut their ski teeth here.

Steamboat has an excellent ski school, of course, which operates 2 miles away on Mt. Werner. But it also has a Ski Club and even a Ski Marching Band. The latter unfurls every February oom-pah-oompah during the ◆ **Steamboat Springs Winter Carnival,** one of the country's oldest ski festivals. It features skijoring and ski obstacle races and ski jumping and skiing with torches and ski parades and ski balls.

At last, in the 1960s, the town was discovered by tourism, first by a giant Texas conglomerate, then by some private investors. In 1981 the real boom began with a Sheraton Convention Hotel.

Millions of dollars have since been invested in new ski lifts, new trails (and reshaping old ones), and other amenities. A Swiss gondola's eight-passenger car, the Silver Bullet, carries loads of skiers an hour up Thunderhead Mountain.

While downhill skiing is taught on a big scale here, cross-country skiing isn't neglected. The many programs even include a Citizens Cross-Country Race Camp for would-be competitors, many of them in their fifties and sixties.

The ◆ **Scandinavian Lodge** has expensive rates, which seem commensurate with its facilities and prestige. For more information write Box 774484, Steamboat Springs 80477, or call (303) 879–0517.

Steamboat does have springs. A walking tour downtown will take you past ten hot springs, with their pungent smell. The largest, harnessed for your pleasure, is at Heart Spring Health and Recreation Center at 136 Lincoln Avenue; (303) 879–1828. For a more natural soak, drive or take a shuttle 8 miles out of town to Strawberry Park Hot Springs, (303) 879–0342.

Steamboat Springs is also home to one of the country's best

The Silver Bullet, Steamboat Springs

automobile driving schools. But don't expect to learn to parallel park here. The ✦**Jean-Paul Luc Winter Driving School** is patterned after similar facilities at European Ski Resorts. Luc is a former race driver with impressive credentials, such as winning the two-wheel class in the Paris-to-Dakar rally.

His school operates from Thanksgiving to mid-March. The track is a 1-mile snow- and ice-covered course with enough turns, loops, and straights to satisfy anyone who likes to play race-car driver.

But this is not play. You often share your class with law-enforcement officers and ambulance personnel. Although these people are professional drivers, they recognize the need for practice, and many return every year. But the novice is welcome here, too. A recent winter student was a homemaker from Atlanta, Georgia, who had never seen snow before.

For safety the track is surrounded by high walls of soft snow. In case of a spin-out—and there will be spin-outs!—the snow guard walls catch the car and hold it safely. No injury to driver or machine.

All vehicles are new and supplied by the school in conjunction with Jeep/Eagle, Michelin, and The Weather Channel. Students are put into threatening positions and must learn how to stop on glare ice on a downhill slope and what to do when the car spins out of control. (No, you don't apply the brake for this one, but the gas, and hard! It works.) After the one-day Ice Immersion class, you will feel confident in your ability to avoid collisions due to ice- and snow-covered roads. Classes available in half-day, full-day, and day-and-a-half sessions. Count on personalized small groups, with video presentations. Prices range from $90 to $340. Instructors remain in constant contact with pupils by two-way radios. These well-qualified teachers monitor every movement from their separate cars, so the students are on their own. For more information call the school at (303) 879–6104 or Steamboat Central Reservations at (800) 922–2722. Mailing address is P.O. Box 774167, Steamboat Springs 80477.

Though Steamboat Springs has grown over the years (permanent year-round population is now 6,000), it has retained its scenic beauty and western charm. Cattle ranching is still important, too. Lots of saddles and boots and Stetsons are for sale in downtown Steamboat.

Those who come to visit or stay are drawn to many of the same qualities that caused James Crawford to settle in the valley.

Steamboat Springs is 170 miles west of Denver via US40. For information on year-round Steamboat Springs, write or call Steamboat Springs Chamber/Resort Association, Steamboat Springs 80488; (303) 879–0740 or (800) 922–2722.

The ◆**Vista Verde Guest & Ski Touring Ranch** sits at the end of a rugged road, 30 miles north of Steamboat Springs, Colorado. It's one of the best such vacation places in the state. The staff is warm, helpful, eager to please, and experienced. Apart from horseback riding, this dude ranch offers supervised hiking, cycling, fly-fishing, and even rock-climbing instruction. Almost every Thursday ballon rides zoom the guests heavenward. In winter you can cross-country ski here.

The summer staff consists of eighteen people who take care of

84

the horses, the housekeeping, the office, and the kitchen, plus hiking guides. Every spring the application letters cascade onto owner John Munn's desk. Munn gets from 200 to 300 applications for the eighteen summer jobs.

The hiring procedure is by telephone—long interviews and reference checks. What does Munn look for? "The work ethic," he says. "The love of the outdoors. Real caring for the guests." Much of the staff is versatile and interchangeable; the Vista Verde's bookkeeper, for instance, helps clean the rooms. The staff brings a good background to the job (Cheryl W., for instance, has worked with horse breeders and horse trainers).

The typical wrangler knows how to shoe horses, knows how to treat the sick ones and please the others. He or she knows a dozen horse tricks. One Oklahoman is so much around the hoofed creatures—his real love—that he has been stepped on, backed into, and severely kicked by horses. A few years ago three of his ribs were broken by one of his animals. The rancher spent a week in the hospital, cursing and cussing. Yet he wouldn't give it all up for anything. His nostrils love the sweet smell of hay and manure, and his ears like to pick up the comforting, caressing sound of horses feeding.

John Munn, the owner, bought the 600-acre former homestead with the environment in mind: He immediately buried the power lines and other utilities underground to enhance the beauty of the high-altitude landscape. Guests sleep in a dozen authentic log cabins. John's wife personally decorated these spacious units.

Shortly after dawn the Vista Verde's Steve A. (the chief wrangler) and Cheryl W. (a "horse person") headed up the hill past the golden aspen trees to the pasture where the horses grazed. "Time for the corral!" Steve A. told them, as though the creatures could understand. Later, the horses saddled, the red-shirted dude ranch staff helped the guests to mount for a morning ride. To Steve A.'s surprise this group of ten new arrivals had lots of riding experience. He trotted ahead, cantering along the winding trail. The western sky was perfectly blue, and a smell of sage was in the air. The colored mountains ascended gently toward more forests. "Lucky you," one of the guests said to the head wrangler. "Spending your summers up here!"

Vista Verde Guest & Ski Touring Ranch, P.O. Box 465, Steamboat Springs 80477; (303) 879–3858 or (800) 526–7433.

85

SOUTHERN COLORADO

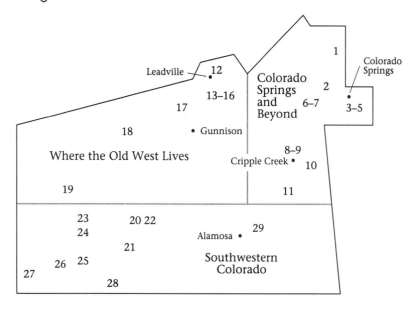

1. Devil's Head Trail
2. Renaissance Festival
3. ProRodeo Hall of Champions and Museum
4. Garden of the Gods
5. Broadmoor
6. Seven Falls
7. Pikes Peak Cog Railway
8. District Museum
9. Mollie Kathleen Gold Mine
10. Pueblo
11. Royal Gorge
12. Camp Hale
13. National Mining Hall of Fame
14. Opera House
15. Matchless Mine Cabin
16. H. A. W. Tabor Home
17. Crested Butte
18. Black Canyon of the Gunnison
19. Basques
20. Pagosa Springs
21. Treasure Falls
22. Chimney Rock
23. Tamarron Resort
24. San Juan National Forest
25. Durango-Silverton Narrow Gauge Train
26. Mesa Verde National Park
27. Hovenweep National Monument
28. Southern Ute and Mountain Ute Reservations
29. Great Sand Dunes National Monument

Southern Colorado

Colorado Springs and Beyond

Contrary to rumors, mountain driving is not especially dangerous or tricky. According to the Colorado State Patrol, most accidents actually happen in the flat, straight stretches at high speeds.

But the stranger to winter is better off knowing a few special driving precautions and tricks. Hence, some thoughts are in order here:

- When renting a car in winter, insist on special snow tires, even if the pavement is dry. Also, better to carry tire chains unnecessarily than to be caught without them when they are essential. Front-wheel drive is preferable for better traction.
- Before starting out on any extended trip in wintertime, the following safety equipment should be checked: brakes, headlights and taillights, exhaust system, windshield wipers, defrosters, heaters, and tools.
- Starting slowly on snow provides better traction and prevents spinning of wheels or skidding sideways into parked cars or other vehicles or objects. On a slick surface start in second gear; this keeps the car's wheels from spinning.
- When driving in a fog or snowstorm, you get better visibility by using the lower headlight beam. The upper headlight beam tends to reflect back off the fog and blind you.
- Whenever visibility becomes so poor, due to fog or snow, that it is impossible to see more than a few feet ahead, you are best to pull off the road. Clean the windshield or wait until the weather eases up.
- Car heaters draw in fresh air from the outside. Cars should never be parked directly behind another car that has the motor running.
- When roads are wet and the temperature drops to 32°F or below, the surface will become icy. Extreme caution is indicated. A single driver can start a chain of mass collisions on ice.
- Get the feel of the road when pavements are slippery by trying brakes occasionally while driving slowly and away from traffic.
- As the temperature rises, ice (and, to a lesser degree, snow) becomes much slicker. For example, at 20 miles per hour when

the temperature is 32°F, stopping distance on ice without tire chains or snow tires is 250 feet. When the temperature is at zero, stopping distance is 110 feet. The difference of 140 feet might well cause a serious accident.

- By stopping slowly, the driver can prevent skidding and come to a safer halt. If your vehicle starts to skid or the wheels lock, release the brake pressure. Pump the brakes; that is, apply the brakes lightly and *intermittently.* A minimum of pressure should be used. Steady, even braking does the trick. Or do you have ABS or disk brakes? If so, just increase the pressure steadily until your car slows down.

- Keep your windshield and windows clear, making sure you can see danger in time to avoid trouble. Windshield-wiper blades should not be too worn; they should be up to the task of removing rain or snow without streaking. Also, the defroster should function efficiently. Ensure good visibility in the rear by removing the snow and ice from the back window when necessary.

- Occasionally a patch of ice will remain on a curve or other shaded spot after the rest of the road has cleared. Be on the lookout for these ice patches.

- A thorough check of the exhaust system should be made at regular intervals; possible leaks could cause a tragedy. (Carbon monoxide poisoning is a deadly driving hazard during wintertime.) It is a good idea to leave at least one window open when driving in cold weather.

- Weather and road conditions in Colorado's mountains are subject to abrupt changes. It is possible to get a report that a certain area is clear, yet you arrive there two or three hours later to find a snowstorm in progress or the highways icy and snow covered. The reverse is also true, and adverse weather conditions often clear up in a short time.

The ◆ **Devil's Head Trail,** in the Rampart Range west of the little community of Sedalia (south of Denver), is one of the state's most scenic trails. It got its name from the red rock formation that sticks out like two horns. You walk up through deep pine forests interspersed with aspen, past giant red cliffs. The trail's length—just 1⅜ miles—doesn't sound like much; it climbs steeply, though, and includes a 1,000-foot vertical elevation gain. (The summit is at 9,747 feet, the parking lot at 8,800 feet.)

89

Along the way you get views of the "fourteeners" (peaks over 14,000 feet high) and the Great Plains. Benches line the uphill paths for the tired. Motorized vehicles (including trail bikes) are outlawed in the ascent to Devil's Head.

Driving directions? From Denver take Sante Fe (US85) south to Sedalia (13 miles); turn west toward Deckers (SR67) for 10 miles and make another left turn onto the Rampart Range Road (County Road 5) another 10 miles until you see the Devil's Head sign.

Joy cometh from hiking!

En route from Denver to Colorado Springs via the interstate highway, you may see a modest sign, LARKSPUR. Few travelers have ever heard of it. Even some Denverites are unfamiliar with this hamlet.

Yet on weekends mid-June through July, tiny Larkspur comes alive with a bang. Cannon shots can be heard from afar. When your car draws closer to the hillside, the cannons are followed by medieval trumpets, in unison.

For almost twenty years the zany, lively ◆**Renaissance Festival** has entertained families in its offbeat location above Larkspur on a wooded Colorado hillside, part theater, part learning experience, part petting zoo for children, part commerce. The Renaissance theme begins when you enter the walled compound and you're greeted as "My Lord" or "My Lady." Artisans galore demonstrate their craft: blacksmiths hammer away, glass blowers regale onlookers with their art, potters have brought their wheels, leather workers show their stuff. Bands of costumed musicians wander up the mountainside. Harpists, flutists, bagpipers, and minstrel singers materialize and harmonize.

Several times a day "King Henry" and his "Court" introduce you to knights jousting on horseback at a gallop, doing tricks with their lances. The stages are busy with storytellers and merrymakers; the pubs dispense barrels of beer and huge turkey legs. Processions of celebrities—Shakespeare, Queen Boleyn—march among the visitors while, a few yards away, you can be a medieval archer or knife thrower or dart artist. Encounter the unexpected: Youngsters ride real camels and elephants; a few steps away jugglers and puppet masters dazzle the onlookers. A good time is had by everyone.

All this against the backdrop of—and amid—Colorado's mountains. The entrance fee is $10. No charge for parking. To reach Larkspur, take exit 172 from I–25. Phone: (303) 688–6010.

What? A *cowboy* museum? A museum with a rodeo theme? Yep, indeed, and it's a sizable one—a concept you won't encounter anywhere else in Colorado but in Colorado Springs, not far from the U.S. Air Force Academy and off the same I–25 highway.

The cowboy played a vital role in opening the West to the expansion of the nineteenth century, and his reputation for courage and individualism has become part of our national folklore and has shaped our character as Americans.

The ◆ **ProRodeo Hall of Champions and Museum** presents this unique heritage in a facility that is both entertaining and educational.

This makes it a fine family destination. The museum offers an outdoor corral with live animals, which always delights children. Inside you learn a lot through dioramas and exhibits of well-displayed saddles, boots, buckles, spurs, ropes, chaps, branding equipment, and other paraphernalia. Rodeo as a sport comes alive through the histories and mementos of America's major rodeo champions.

The visitor can learn about such colorful rodeo champs as bull rider Warren G. "Freckles" Brown, reputed to be the oldest man in ProRodeo history to win a riding event. His long career was interrupted by a broken neck as well as by World War II. With typical spirit during wartime parachute jumps into China, Brown put on a rodeo using army mules and native cattle and declared himself the Orient's all-around champion of 1942.

Rodeo began after the long cattle drives of the mid-1800s when cowboys gathered informally to let off steam competing against each other in the everyday skills of the cowhand—roping, riding, tangling with bucking horses and wild bulls.

Over the years rules and equipment were standardized, judging was streamlined, prize money was increased, and the freewheeling entertainment of the 1800s evolved into the modern sport of professional rodeo.

In 1979 the ProRodeo Museum was opened in Colorado Springs. It captures the flavor and history of rodeo as well as honoring the cowboys, past and present, who created it.

91

Here the visitor can learn the fine points of saddle bronc riding and how to judge a rider's performance and can get the jolting sensation, through film with stereo sound, of what it's like to ride a bucking Brahma bull. Other films trace the historical development of rodeo.

The ProRodeo Hall of Champions is located just north of Colorado Springs on I-25 at exit 147. Hours are 9:00 A.M. to 5:00 P.M. daily, Memorial Day through Labor Day. Winter hours are 9:00 A.M.–4:30 P.M. Tuesday through Saturday; noon–4:30 P.M. Sundays; and closed Mondays. A fee of $5.00 is charged to help defray expenses of the nonprofit museum. Call (719) 528-4764.

The wonders of nature blend together at the ❖ **Garden of the Gods** to create one of the most varied natural settings in Colorado. Established as a free city park in 1909, the almost 1,370 acres are filled with silent and spectacular red sandstone rock formations, including Gateway Rocks, Cathedral Spires, and the Balanced Rock. Grasslands meet mountain forests to provide contrasts of scenic beauty.

A common resident of the park is the great horned owl, whose keen light-gathering eyes and superior hearing make it an effective nighttime hunter.

Hike, picnic, and horseback ride to fully appreciate the park's natural beauty. But most of all bring your camera and photograph these wonders (especially at sunset or sunrise when the low sun accents the naturally colorful redstone).

Open daily 8:30 A.M.–5:00 P.M., off US24, Colorado Springs.

The five-star ❖ **Broadmoor** is the only major Colorado resort that has 14,100-foot Pikes Peak for a backdrop.

The Broadmoor Resort actually began in the 1850s with a Silesian count. He hoped to create another Monte Carlo against the backdrop of Colorado's mountainscape. Eventually two Philadelphians, Charles Tutt and Spencer Penrose, took over. They'd gotten rich in Cripple Creek mining and real estate; as world travelers, they knew what they wanted: a regal Renaissance-style hotel.

The Broadmoor's doors opened on June 29, 1918; among several notables, the first to register was John D. Rockefeller, Jr. Since that day, there has been a stream of industrialists, diplomats, movie moguls, film stars, and titled ladies and gentlemen. They mingle nicely nowadays with anyone who can afford this pricey year-round retreat. It is the largest, plushest, and most elegant in Colorado, offering every conceivable amenity.

The (deluxe) Broadmoor isn't for economy travelers; bring lots of traveler's checks or your best credit card—Diner's, American Express, Visa, or MasterCard are acceptable. For more information: The Broadmoor, P.O. Box 1439, Colorado Springs 80901; (719) 634–7711 or (800) 634–7711.

◆ **Seven Falls** is ten driving minutes west of the Broadmoor resort. "The Grandest Mile of Scenery in Colorado" lives up to its slogan: A 1,000-foot-high granite canyon leads to seven waterfalls flanked by healthy forests of juniper, blue spruce, Douglas fir, and ponderosa pine. Not far from the dramatic, perpendicular "pillars of Hercules," you can climb several hundred steep steps to platforms from which you view these scenic wonders.

You get to Seven Falls via Cheyenne Boulevard and Mesa. For more information: Box 118, Colorado Springs 80901; (719) 632–0752.

The year was 1806; the discoverer of Colorado Springs's "Great Mountain" was Lieutenant Zebulon Montgomery Pike. Neither he nor any of his party got even close to the summit due to bad weather and perhaps a lack of planning. At that time it certainly wasn't conceivable that one of America's most unusual railroads ever constructed would carry thousands of persons to its summit.

Today a visit to Colorado Springs can be enhanced by a trip on the country's highest railroad to the summit of famous Pikes Peak. The ◆ **Pikes Peak Cog Railroad,** which is 46,158 feet long, climbs from an elevation of 6,571 feet at the Manitou Springs station to one of 14,110 feet at the summit. This is a vertical gain of 7,539 feet, or an average of 846 feet per mile. Actually, the distance is longer than any covered by the famous cog-wheel rails in Switzerland.

Along the entire route you'll be treated to a continuous panorama of scenery. At the 11,578-foot level, the trains emerge from a sea of quaking aspen into the windswept stretches of timberline and climb into the Saddle, where you get an unparalleled view of Manitou Springs and of Garden of the Gods in the valley below. You also see the vast expanses of the Great Plains stretch toward the horizon.

On clear days it is possible to spot Denver 75 miles to the north of Colorado Springs and the dramatic Sangre de Cristo Mountains

93

in southern Colorado. The view of the west is astounding; mile upon mile of snowcapped giants rise into the blue Colorado sky. As the Swiss-made train reaches the summit of Pikes Peak, you can walk up to an observation tower on top of the old Summit House, which contains a curio shop, an information desk, and a concession counter for light lunches. (Or bring your own brown bag.)

You reach Manitou Springs from Colorado Springs via US24. Continue west on Manitou Avenue; turn left at Ruxton. The depot is at 515 Ruxton Avenue.

The Pikes Peak Cog Railroad leaves Manitou Springs every three hours from 8:00 A.M. to 5:20 P.M. daily, May–October. Extra trains in July and August. Round-trip is three hours, ten minutes. For reservations call (719) 685–5401 in Manitou Springs.

Back in 1891 the Cripple Creek gold strike proved to be the last major gold rush in North America. Within a few years those mines in the mountains west of Colorado Springs yielded almost a billion dollars' worth of the valuable mineral. By 1900 Cripple Creek grew to some 50,000 inhabitants. The miners could patronize seventy-five saloons, forty grocery stores, seventeen churches, and eight newspapers. Every day a dozen passenger trains steamed into the depot.

Eventually 500 gold mines operated in the area. Some 8,000 men brought on a gambling, carousing, whoring boom.

Cripple Creek! Ironically, the man who discovered the first gold vein sold his claim for $500 and proceeded to drink it all up. Colorado Springs owes part of its existence to the prospectors. In time celebrities came and went. Adventurer Lowell Thomas was born in nearby Victor, now a near–ghost town. Groucho Marx once drove a grocery wagon in Cripple Creek. Jack Dempsey, for a brief bout a miner, trained and boxed in the region. Financier Bernard Baruch worked as a telegrapher here. Teddy Roosevelt, after a Cripple Creek visit, told the world that "the scenery bankrupts the English language." The politicians arrived in droves to see for themselves.

By and by, gold prices dropped. Production began to slip. The miners scattered. By 1920 fewer than 5,000 people lived here.

And today? Cripple Creek attracts some 225,000 summer tourists. They come for the narrow-gauge train rides. They pan for gold right on Main Street. They attend one of the twelve weekly summer performances of the classic, professional melodrama

Abandoned mine, Cripple Creek

at the Imperial Hotel. Call (719) 689–2922 for information about dates and times, which can change.

The old railroad depot has become the ◆ **District Museum.** Three stories are crammed with mementos of the mining age. Superbly kept up, the museum is well worth a visit. Hours: daily 10:00 A.M.–5:00 P.M. Memorial Day through September; weekends for the rest of the year. Call (719) 689–2634.

The local folks are calmly friendly despite the tourist hubbub. Cripple Creek jumps with visitors all summer. They flock to the red brick souvenir and antiques shops, where a 1929 beer bottle or a 1950s glass pitcher sells as if it were a rare treasure. You can watch the donkeys on Bennett Avenue, buy cowboy boots in a real western store, and eat home-cooked food in little cafes. Main

Street bustles with some shops that sell tacky merchandise. The cars jostle for a place to park.

Not many travelers venture on foot beyond the central core of this community. Yet visual rewards await those who make the most of Cripple Creek's lovely location. It is nestled among the Colorado hillsides, which climb from town (elevation: a high 9,494 feet) in every direction. Nature awaits the walker who leaves the red brick confines and heads for the slopes of conifers and aspen trees. The mountains here are studded with old mines, which you reach by hiking up the abandoned roads past rusting machinery, past the old wooden mine trestles, past the piles of forgotten ore. The ✦**Mollie Kathleen Gold Mine** still attracts paying visitors, who can tour the mine.

Cripple Creek deserves more than a few hasty hours. At least one overnight stay makes sense. And recently slot machines and other gaming devices have come to this community. Visitors hope to strike it rich at the Palace Hotel, Long Branch, Diamond Lil's, Wild Bill's, Brass Ass, Silver Palace, Gold Rush, Imperial Hotel, Maverick's, or Wild Wild West.

Cripple Creek is 45 miles west of Colorado Springs. From there it can be reached via US24 west, then SR67. The Chamber of Commerce address: Box 650, Cripple Creek 80813 (719–689–2169).

The trip will be a memorable one.

On your drive to southern Colorado, you may want to stop in ✦**Pueblo,** a quiet, hospitable community of 125,000 souls who, in recent years, have gone historic. The citizenry is especially proud of its Union Avenue Historic District. The area's walking tour concentrates on about two dozen restored edifices of the 1840s to 1890s: the Fort Pueblo (1842), at 324 West First Street; the Union Depot (1889), at 132 West B Street; the Holden Block (1883), named after Pueblo's first mayor; plus many others. These brick buildings have been hardly publicized yet are worth seeing. In a nearby residential district, there awaits one of Colorado's most stately bed-and-breakfasts; this mansion is known as the Abriendo Inn (300 West Abriendo Avenue, Pueblo 81004; (719) 544-2703. This distinguished small hostelry couldn't have a better location, not far from the community college and the historic Union Avenue. The inn has only seven rooms, each a little different but all with period furniture, old-fashioned lace curtains, canopied or brass beds, fresh flowers, oak antiques, and original art. Intriguingly, each room comes with appropriate magazines like *Victorian Homes, Country Living,* and *Architectural Digest.* The owner happens to be an interior designer and noted gourmet whose staff dishes up free evening snacks and unexpected breakfast inventions. The aristocratic atmosphere makes one think of an embassy; in fact, the inn is so perfect that it's slightly intimidating. (The grandeur is inexpensive, however; a night at the Abriendo Inn costs about one-half of Grand Hotel accommodations.) Pueblo Information Line: (719) 542–1704.

 ◆Royal Gorge! The 1,200-foot-deep canyon fetches more than 500,000 sightseers a year. Travelers plumb the rocky canyon depths via a steep incline railway or drive across a mighty suspension bridge—allegedly the world's highest—or see it all from the bottom as railroad passengers.

There is also the tram.

Like similar ones in Stateline, California, and Sandia Peak, New Mexico, the Royal Gorge tram cabin is painted a fire-red. It takes thirty-five passengers. A guide-conductor will assure any timid riders that the tram will not fall into the Arkansas River, which runs way below. "We have three braking systems," the conductor will say, "and an extra motor, just in case." In the terminals about one hundred tons of concrete and steel anchor the big cables for the conveyance.

It took a helicopter to string the pilot cable. It also took $350,000 of good Texas money to rig up this Colorado tourist attraction.

All of this adds up to a clever accumulation of conversation pieces for out-of-state visitors. First of all, you have the canyon itself. It has been compared to the Grand Canyon. The colors are reds, mauves, yellows, and browns. The chasm is so deep that it stopped Lieutenant Zebulon Pike in 1806. He just couldn't make it across. (Pikes Peak was named after him, although he didn't scale that one, either.)

By 1878, after a lot of fighting between two railroads, engineers had built their tracks along the river. Then in 1929 ladies in long fur coats and their escorts in ancient automobiles drove up to see the sensation of the year, the Royal Gorge Bridge. It's still there, six decades later.

You can drive across the wooden planks or even hike over to the other side. In addition, you can step into one of the Incline Railway cars and slowly rumble down to the Arkansas River. The five-minute ride is deafening because you always have many excited children aboard.

97

The Incline conveyance dates back to the early thirties. During the sixties the promoters bought an additional family satisfier. This is a little scale-model train, a replica of an 1863 Southern Pacific. The train chugs around the Royal Gorge Park. Along the way you may see deer, trees, cacti, bushes, and miles of granite. Royal Gorge also contains various nature trails. Films are sold at the visitor center, from where you can send postcards with the "Royal Gorge, Colorado" postmark. Other people like to send home a picture of Point Sublime, depicting many caves, craters, and rock slabs.

The myriad amusements are open all year. The charges for the various modes of transportation are reasonable. Or you can try it all without paying. Just bring a long rock-climbing rope, a solid pair of boots, and enough expertise to get down a perpendicular 1,200-foot rock.

The Royal Gorge is located 8 miles west of Canon City via US50. Canon City is southwest of Colorado Springs and west of Pueblo. For information: Royal Gorge Scenic Railway, Box 549, Canon City 81212; (719) 275–7507.

WHERE THE OLD WEST LIVES

Camp Hale was nicknamed "Camp Hell" by the Mountain Troopers, who first trained here, 18 miles north of Leadville. From 1942 to 1945 the camp served the famous World War II Tenth Mountain Division. Much of their tough battle preparations took place at the chilly 9,500 feet above sea level, on 6,500 mountain acres, surrounded by 12,000-foot snow giants.

The altitude and the thin air took their toll on young recruits from the Midwest; the new arrivals couldn't sleep at first and felt weak during the day. Smoke from 300 barrack chimneys and railroads hung over the camp, and you could hear a lot of coughing.

Camp Hale days often started at 4:30 A.M. with 15-mile marches through blizzards. Packs weighed eighty pounds or more, and the troopers would be pulled backward. The army skis were often so stiff that they sank into the snow. Some southern and midwestern fellows, recruited at the last minute, termed skis their "torture boards." Each time a novice lifted a leg, his muscles hurt. The arms ached, too, from the unaccustomed efforts. The Camp Hale–based mountain warfare soldiers were made to climb 12,000-foot peaks on skis while the temperature could fall to 20° below zero.

To get these men ready for combat against German *Gebirgsjäger* troops, the U.S. Army made even the basic training as realistic as possible. For a Camp Hale "Infiltration Course," the troopers had to crawl under barbed wire for an hour. The, suddenly, machine guns with live shells shot directly over their heads. Fifty-pound charges of dynamite blew up right and left. Occasional mistakes would cause actual injuries.

Life at Camp Hale was never monotonous; the Tenth Mountain Division troops were employed to test Arctic snow vehicles and battle-station rescue toboggans. Troopers trained on large snowshoes and learned how to control avalanches. Other men worked with mules and dogs. A Scandinavian explorer was invited to teach the soldiers how to build igloos and other snow caves. Some of the camp's crack skiers and instructors were actually well-known ski racers or ski jumpers like Walter Prager and Torger Tokle; others like Gordon Wren and Steve Knowlton joined U.S. Olympic ski teams after World War II.

The training of these soldiers turned even tougher in February 1944, when the Tenth Mountain men were sent on their first "D-series" maneuvers. They climbed Colorado's Tennessee Pass and moved for thirty days into the icy wilderness. Snows were so deep that supply vehicles couldn't get through. Loads were so heavy (up to ninety pounds) that only the best troopers could make it. Despite the 35°-below-zero temperatures, no fires were allowed. After devouring K-rations, the food ran out. The struggling Tenth ate almost nothing for three days. When they got back to Hale, there were one hundred frostbite cases. Nearby hospitals filled with pneumonia victims.

In summer the soldiers received instruction in advanced rock-climbing techniques; they rappelled down the sheer Colorado cliffs and had to walk on suspended cables and rain-wet logs. Mountaineering knowledge would come in handy. In November 1944 the division left Camp Hale for Italy, where the troopers distinguished themselves in battling the Germans.

And the camp in Colorado? For a time Camp Hale housed German POWs. After the latter went home, the flagpoles, mule barns, and other buildings were forgotten. Suddenly, in 1947 the Pentagon brass decided to send other young soldiers to try the

Colorado snows for size. Like the former Camp Hale occupants, these infantrymen pitted themselves against winter cold. When the Korean War broke out in 1950, Camp Hale served the Rangers as a special training ground. A few years later army helicopters got their battle tests here. By then ski troopers no longer seemed as necessary as during World War II days, and most of the military skiing moved out of Colorado and north to Alaska. On July 1, 1965, the buglers sounded a last Camp Hale retreat. Afterward the U.S. Forest Service once more took control of the area.

During the late 1970s the Forest Service invested money and time to build the Camp Hale picnic areas, hiking paths, a wheelchair trail, and parking spaces at the one-time training camp. In May 1980 many former troopers came up for the dedication of the twenty-acre Camp Hale Memorial Campground. It is one of the highest such sites in the United States.

Not far away from camp on Tennessee Pass, a fourteen-ton slab of granite reaches 20 feet into the sky. The stone's Roll of Honor lists the 990 comrades who gave their lives for the division. Each year on Memorial Day, hundreds of ex-troopers assemble at Tennessee Pass to remember their companions. Later they get together to talk about the old days, to swap tales, or to present their families to one another.

Camp Hale, now a U.S. Forest Service Campground, is 180 miles west of Denver via I–70 and SR91.

This is a story of love and power, of wealth and poverty, of joys and tragedy, of a Colorado mining town whose fortunes flourished and vanished. A story so extraordinary that it became the subject of an opera, a play, and many biographies, some of them bad ones.

The characters were bigger than life. Begin with Horace Austin Warner Tabor, a one-time Vermont stonecutter, and his straight-laced hardworking wife Augusta. The couple gave up a Kansas homestead to try their luck first in Denver, then under Pikes Peak, then at Oro City. They arrived in Leadville with a rickety wagon and an old ox during the 1860s, some years after the first gold had been discovered in California Gulch.

The Tabors established themselves as best as they could—Augusta with a tiny roominghouse and a small bakery, Horace with a store and later a part-time job as mayor.

The Tabors' first break came on April 20, 1878. Two destitute miners, new in town, dropped into Horace's shop. Could he help out with some tools and a basket of groceries? The accommodating mayor agreed to help for a third of whatever minerals they might find. A few days later some hard digging produced a rich silver vein.

The Tabors were launched. By summer that first mine—the Little Pittsburgh—lavished $8,000 a week on its owners. Before long there was $100,000 worth of silver per month; this was followed by other Tabor ventures, all successful. In time he invested in many mines, owned a good chunk of the local bank, built the Leadville Opera House, and erected mansions in the mining town and in Denver. He owned a lot of real estate and a hotel. By 1879 Leadville had seventeen independent smelters; it took 2,000 lumberjacks to provide enough wood to fire the machinery that processed the silver riches. Thanks to Tabor's new wealth and almost daily discoveries of more ore, the immigrants flooded to Leadville in droves. Celebrities like the "Unsinkable" Molly Brown showed up, as did various Dows, Guggenheims, and Boettchers.

Marshall Sprague, a western mining authority, describes in *Money Mountain* the hustle and bustle when thousands streamed across the Continental Divide to Leadville. The road was "jammed with wagons, stages, buggies, carts. There were men pushing wheelbarrows, men riding animals, men and dogs driving herds of cattle, sheep, pigs and goats."

Tabor soon bought an additional mine—the Matchless. He prospered while Leadville grew to a city of 30,000. Oscar Wilde appeared in Tabor's famous Opera House. The Chicago Symphony Orchestra and the Metropolitan Opera came there, to faraway Colorado. Well-known singers, ballet dancers, actresses, and entertainers arrived to perform.

H. A. W. Tabor became a millionaire many times over. He was a tall man, mustached, kindly, and, as a local historian writes, "outgoing, gregarious, and honest as the falling rain." By contrast, Horace was married to an unloving woman who, although she worked hard, brought Tabor no happiness. She nagged; she was prim and humorless. Colorado's richest man thought he deserved better.

Horace Tabor's luck changed one day in 1882. That evening the fifty-year-old silver magnate saw Elisabeth Doe-McCourt in the restaurant of Leadville's Clarendon Hotel.

"Baby" Doe was twenty-two—a beauty with shining blue eyes

and curly dark blond hair. Round-faced and charming, she'd been born into an Irish immigrant family of fourteen children. Baby Doe had just emerged from a brief, unhappy marriage with an unsupportive miner in Central City. Recently divorced, she had the good sense to look for a better partner in booming Leadville. She was a respectable young woman. And her search was crowned by success.

What began as a simple flirtation deepened into an abiding love that scandalized the Rockies and became the celebrated story of Colorado's opera the *Ballad of Baby Doe,* by Broadway veterans John Latouche and Douglas Moore.

Horace and Baby Doe were snubbed by Denver High Society when Tabor divorced his cold wife, Augusta, who allegedly received a $500,000 settlement. H. A. W. soon married his new love. The wedding took place in Washington, D.C., in the presence of President Chester Arthur and other dignitaries. Baby Doe received a $90,000 diamond necklace, and she wore a $7,500 gown.

Although young, she actually had greater substance than most of her biographers gave her credit for. She was honest and loyal, helpful to others, and interested in a variety of things. Best of all, she was in love with her much older Colorado husband. Her love was returned.

The Tabors lived the lavish life of luxury to the hilt. Most historians estimate that the Tabors spent some $100 million. Horace Tabor made few worthwhile investments. For a brief time he was elected to the U.S. Senate.

In 1893 disaster struck Leadville. Silver was replaced by paper money. The nation experienced a financial panic.

The Tabors were ruined. The mines began to fail. Real estate was sold to satisfy creditors.

The couple moved to Denver, still deeply in love. Thanks to some contacts, Horace got a postmaster's job for a short time. But the financial plunge must have been too much for him. Soon he was ailing. His final hours came on April 10, 1899, at Denver's Windsor Hotel. His wife, Baby Doe, was by his side, holding his hand.

Before Horace Tabor died, he once more spoke about his Matchless Mine in Leadville. It had long played out after yielding some $1 million during its fourteen years of operation. "Hold on to the Matchless," Tabor whispered. "It'll make millions again." His wife nodded.

Baby Doe kept her promise. She moved back to Leadville. Penniless, she lived in a shack beside the mine pit for thirty-six years. She remained faithful to Tabor.

During the winter of 1935, while in her seventies, she shopped at a local grocery for some food. The grocer gave her a ride home in his truck. She was dressed in tatters. Her feet were sheathed in sackcloth instead of shoes. The cabin next to the Matchless Mine was squalid, but she kept a rifle in it, protecting her mine.

Leadville's altitude is more than 10,000 feet. It gets cold there on winter nights. Baby Doe Tabor was found in her shack on March 7, 1935. She had frozen to death. No one knows how long the body had been there. Ironically, there were some unopened boxes with new blankets sent by some Leadville sympathizers, which the dying woman had refused to use. Pride.

The Tabors are buried side by side in Denver. The *Ballad of Baby Doe* was added to the New York City Opera's repertoire shortly after its 1956 debut in Central City, Colorado. The role of Baby Doe was among the first that the then newcomer Beverly Sills sang for a company she was to head many years later.

And how about the current Leadville? Thanks to Leadville's solid mining history, there is a 70,000-square-foot ◆**National Mining Hall of Fame.** This museum should be essential for ore seekers, mining school students, and history buffs. Located in a restored Victorian schoolhouse, the facility retraces the entire Leadville history; you can also view old equipment, assorted rocks and crystals, various artifacts, and dioramas.

A recent addition, "The Last Chance," is a realistic replica of a hard-rock mine tunnel. Stretching over 120 feet, the "rock" walls have exposed ore veins. Mine-gauge rail tracks are underfoot on the rock-strewn floor. Dripping water adds to the illusion of being underground in a real mine. Small admission charge. Contact the National Mining Hall of Fame & Museum, 120 West Ninth Street, Leadville 80461-0981; (719) 486–1229.

The city has seen three decades of modest restoration, and you notice many red brick buildings on Main Street. Tabor's ◆**Opera House** still stands. The tiny ◆**Matchless Mine Cabin** has become a minimuseum. The original ◆**H. A. W. Tabor Home,** where he lived with Augusta, can be visited by tourists. Unfortunately, the Leadville city leaders do not support interest in history during the winter months.

The Tabor sites are closed from Labor Day to Memorial Day. Leadville can be reached from Denver by I–70 and the Copper Mountain turnoff. For more information: Leadville–Lake County Chamber of Commerce, P.O. Box 891, Leadville 80461: (719) 486–3900 or (800) 933–3901.

◆ **Crested Butte** is a sizable, scenic ski center, thirty minutes north of Gunnison, Colorado, too far from the big metropolitan cities to attract crowds. (Denver is 235 miles to the northeast.) One local inhabitant explains Crested Butte this way: "In an age plagued by problems of too many people, too many cars and roads and buildings, this kind of country has a special attraction. It seems to have been made *for* people, not *by* them."

Crested Butte aficionados speak of a feeling "that borders on reverence, a joy of simply being here." The ski area and the nearby mini–mining town of Crested Butte (2 miles away) give off a feeling of relaxation. The atmosphere is pastoral, sometimes even somnolent, informal, tolerant, nature rooted.

These mountains are some of the state's most beautiful. They combine all the power and grace of the Swiss Alps, and you seem to ski in a never-ending symphony of valleys and meadows, of crests and snowfields. Crested Butte is blessed with nicely separated terrain for experts (only 20 percent of the land), intermediates (55 percent), and beginners (25 percent). Beginners are especially fortunate here.

One of the area's major assets is a gently sloping, broad, chairlift-served run on the lower mountain more than a mile long. It is excellent for novice skiers, who at many areas are confined to short, makeshift slopes with minimal lift facilities. The upper mountain holds myriad pleasures for more advanced skiers. One chairlift, for example, serves slopes with an average grade of 44 percent, which experts find challenging (and which will scare the daylights out of average types).

The larger part of the area is for the intermediate skier. This includes a many-trails complex that taps the open ski terrain of Crested Butte's north-side slopes. Here the snow comes earlier, stays longer, and is deeper and lighter than anywhere else on the mountain, with an average 33 percent grade, 1,350 vertical feet. Ideal for intermediate skiing, the Paradise Bowl reminds one of Vail's bowls and provides great joys to most visitors.

Crested Butte's lift situation is adequate, thanks to a dozen chairlifts. A gondola would be an asset and add prestige.

The ski school has an important and reliable cross-country program for which the surrounding country seems perfectly suited.

Colorado's choicest cross-country adventure—indeed, a special pièce de résistance for experts—ties Crested Butte with Aspen, just 28 miles away (guides available). Rentals are available in town and at the base lodge shop.

Some of the area's ski clientele never saw snow before. The ski school is therefore a patient one. The names of some ski runs give a good clue to the customers—Houston Trail, Kansas Trail. Charters regularly fly in from states like Georgia, and you'll find some midwestern family trade. It is intriguing to simply sit in front of the base cafeteria and watch the mix of people, especially on weekends. Crested Butte draws from the local state college then, and you'll see the tanned, casual, enamored youth in full bloom: pink-cheeked young women, fellows in jeans, jeans, and more jeans.

The town of Crested Butte gets its character from the old mining days, and the streets are full of young and old men with beards, who all look alike. On weekends you glimpse sheriffs with badges, and there are some town drunks to be taken care of. Night life is limited to saloons with loud banjos and other instruments, beer drinking, and talking to the multitude of ski bums. Many dogs sit in front of the clapboard buildings; dogs of various shapes leap across the pockmarked streets or show up at the lived-in ski area. Food and lodging prices range from moderate to expensive. Accommodations are available in old lodges and well-worn guest houses, plus condos for the rich. There is a glossy hotel.

Fat Tire Week in Crested Butte is a summer party on wheels. More than 1,000 people will show up to participate in bicycle polo, races, clinics, and tours that range from mild-mannered wildflower rides to the grinding ascent of 10,500-foot Scofield Pass. With more than 300 miles of trails, Crested Butte has a ride to satisfy every cyclist.

Crested Butte was the site of the first mountain biking in Colorado. After a motorcycle gang had ridden their Harley Davidsons over the rough jeep road of Pearl Pass from Aspen, some "Butte" locals decided to one-up the bikers by doing the same route on bicycles.

Mountain biking was born.

Since then these bikes have evolved from one-speed clunkers into technological wonders of metal and gears. Crested Butte continues to celebrate this development with the Mountain Biking Hall of Fame and Museum.

Mountain bikes were designed to act like jeeps for going over rough terrain. Tires are big, fat, and knobby for climbing through gravel and maintaining traction on a steep grade. As opposed to the racing type of road bikes with skinny tires designed for maximum speed, mountain bikes have anywhere from eighteen to twenty-one gears. This allows you to shift way down to what is called a "granny gear" and, moving at slow speeds, still be able to pedal up and over obstacles. By turning your pedals as quickly as possible—called "spinning"—you ensure that the gears absorb the load, rather than your knees.

Mountain bikes take some getting used to. Riding a trail over rocks and logs and through streams can be a bit intimidating. Be prepared to take a few falls at first.

One way to avoid crashing into obstacles like rocks is to look for a path around them instead of focusing on what is in your path. The technique of keeping your eye on the ball in tennis can be applied to mountain biking. By concentrating on the tennis ball, you are almost assured of hitting it. By eyeballing that obstacle in your trail, you will hit it, too. Keep looking up the trail, not just in front of you. Like a skier, you have to anticipate your next move.

To maintain traction while going down a steep hill, stand up in the pedals and stick your rear end behind the bike seat for more weight on the back tire. Also, brake most firmly with the rear brake. Using your front brake alone can abruptly stop the front tire and send you flying over the handlebars in what is called an "endo" (rear end flips over the front). A very undignified way to get off a bike.

Required equipment includes a helmet, eye protection, cycling gloves, and shorts to prevent chafing of inner thighs. Drink from your water bottle frequently to avoid dehydration.

Most of the trails you will ride are open to public use. Cyclists are required to yield to hikers and horses. If this means you have to get off your bike and move off the trail, then do it. In many parts of the United States, failure of cyclists to yield has caused some popular trails to be closed to them. Be considerate of others and the environment.

Following on the wheels of Fat Tire Week is the Crested Butte Wildflower Festival. Of course, all mountain towns have wildflowers, but the climate of sheltered valleys seems to provide more floral color here than anywhere else. The town also does its best to make sure everyone can enjoy these delicate blooms. Days of naturalist walks, tours, photo sessions, painting classes with professional outdoor artists, evening dinners, lunch discussions, horseback tours into the higher meadows, and ski-lift rides to the top of the ski area for a leisurely walk down are some of the offerings. Variable fees for each activity help support the organizers of the event. Posters, books, and varied artwork are on sale. This a low-key celebration of the natural mountain beauty. Many of the activities are well suited to children or to people who like to move along at a slow pace. For others, the guides will match your speed.

Crested Butte is a thirty-minute drive north of Gunnison on SR135. For more information: Crested Butte, P.O. Box A, Mt. Crested Butte 81225; (800) 544–8448, (800) 525–4220, or (303) 349–6438.

East of Montrose US50 cuts through fields of alfalfa and corn. Then the road begins to curve and climb. After 15 miles you see the visitor center.

Suddenly, you are face to face with the ◆**Black Canyon of the Gunnison.** You hear the roar of the Gunnison River 2,700 feet below.

The vision of the sheer, massive rocks is stunning and unforgettable. In the sunlight the black granite turns a mauve color. Towers, pillars, and stone blocks scintillate and make humans feel tiny. In all, the Black Canyon of the Gunnison National Monument comprises some 20,800 acres. Carved by the river, the canyon is 53 miles long.

The South Rim offers excellent access on the well-maintained SR347. Rangers answer questions and lead hikes. The trails are steep. They're shaded by scrub oak; on your descent toward the Gunnison River, you see white daisies, violet asters, mariposa lilies, yarrow, and lupine lilies. Chipmunks and squirrels peer out from the vegetation and the rock cracks. Golden eagles fly overhead.

The Chasm View Nature Trail measures a modest ⅓ mile. The North Vista Trail is more ambitious, at 3½ miles, and can be strenuous. A permit is required if you want to hike down all the way to the river. Rock climbing in the canyon is considered hazardous

107

and is only for experienced climbers. (Register at the visitor center.) The National Monument is open in winter as well, with fewer personnel.

For more information write National Park Headquarters, 2233 East Main Street, Montrose 81401, or call (303) 249–7036 on weekdays. If you need accommodations, the luxurious Red Arrow Inn, on US50 in Montrose, is the closest to the Black Canyon of the Gunnison (reservations: 303–249–9641).

Consider the ◆**Basques** who herd sheep in the western U.S. Rockies and whose homeland is the sometimes foggy Pyrenees, mountains that separate Spain from France. Colorado's Basques are not unhappy with their lot. Bernard De Voto once asked a Basque why he chose to live among sheep. "I seek the quiet heart," the shepherd answered.

The "quiet heart" of solitude can be found by these men among the meadows and knolls of their homeland as well as on the hillsides of Colorado. In the United States they are concentrated in and around Montrose and Grand Junction. The herders are in tune with their mountains, which make a "mighty big bedroom," as they like to explain.

Most of the younger Basques are single; for them shearing time and the yearly folk festivals—with dancing, weight lifting, and wine drinking—fill a need. Many of these mountain men own their herds and let the unmarried do the herding while they stick to family life. Whether living in the western U.S. Rockies or in the Pyrenees, the Basques hold onto their own difficult-to-learn language. It resembles none other in Europe and still puzzles philologists.

Colorado's Basques wear the berets and the modest working clothes of their ancestors. Their ethnic origins remain unclear; they seem to have been in Europe longer than other groups. Anthropologists theorize that these dark-complexioned mountain people may have migrated to the Iberian Peninsula from the Caucasus some 2,000 years before Christ. Both the Basque sheep herders and the Basque farmers live modestly and accept their place in the Colorado high country.

SOUTHWESTERN COLORADO

The chute opens and Joe Alexander, champion bareback rider, holds onto the horse's riggings with one hand. The horse rears wildly, resenting the man, hooves in all directions, a bucking, pitching, twisting, snorting wild-eyed rebel. The cowboy's hat flies high, landing in the dust.

He has been on the horse for five seconds now, and he still hangs on. He leans all the way back, ankles still spurring, his shoulder blades against the animal's spine. The man's out-stretched arm hits the horse's bones. It's a human against a beast. Six seconds now. Seven. Eight.

The buzzer sounds. Alexander jumps safely onto the ground.

Eight seconds of bareback riding can seem like eight hours. It still takes a strong, bold person to ride at rodeos.

These Wild West riding competitions are an important income source for some Colorado cowboys. After all, the cattle business in the United States has shrunk during the past decades. Much of the profit has been taken out. These days, ranches are fewer, and, although some of the successful ones are in southern Colorado, they're smaller than they used to be.

At one time hundreds of men were needed to drive 6,000 or more Black Angus, Herefords, Shorthorns, and other breeds to market. Nowadays trucks do the job. The old-time cowhand had to feed the stock in winter—a job often done by helicopters these days.

In sheer numbers the western cowboy has diminished, but a few large Colorado ranches still need these rugged, underpaid men to brand cattle in spring, to put up and repair fences, to rope the creatures, and to look after their health. One ranch man-ager, for a big cattle company thirty minutes south of Denver, still rounds up his stock twice a year. In the saddle for long hours, he enjoys the freedom of his 10,000 acres. He dresses the part, too. Cowboy hat, leather vest, leather belts with elaborate buck-les, Levis, buckaroo boots. He says he enjoys the heat and getting dirty; few people know that he has a law degree.

Many cowboys have learned some of the veterinary skills; they know a lot about the pharmaceuticals and the vaccina-tions of the present-day western cattle industry. Likewise, cow-boys learn about feeding, and they help with cattle sales. A few hardy cowpunchers still ride with their herds from moun-tain pasture to pasture, all summer long. The riders certainly must look after their horses. And Colorado is the state where it all happens.

This leads back to the rodeo circuit, which has become lucrative for some Colorado cowboys of all ages who can travel to more than 1,000 competitions that go on during the year in North America. In addition, there are hundreds of nonsanctioned amateur and intercollegiate rodeos and even some for kids.

Thirty million American tourists travel to the big spectacles. For ten days each July, for instance, many of the Colorado-based cowboys and cattle flock to Calgary, in Canada's province of Alberta, where the purses keep increasing. Altogether some $5 million in prizes go to riders in the United States and Canada; at Wyoming's famous Frontier Days alone, $650,000 in rodeo winnings are split by a cast of 1,500. About 300,000 visitors are entertained here.

The top cowboys often own sizable cattle ranches themselves. The famous ones sometimes fly their own planes.

Rodeo actually began as an exciting pastime of those rough, tough cowhands who rode the range and drove the herds of beef to market. "Ride 'em cowboy" was not much more than a contest of bravery among cowboys of the Old West. From these unassuming beginnings rodeo has evolved into a Big Business.

Some Colorado cowboys (and cowgirls) take care of the horses at dozens of the state's dude ranches. The latter are basically rustic, with western-style furniture against a log cabin backdrop. The rooms often contain fur-covered sofas, rugged granite fireplaces, elk antlers on the walls, or framed words of cowboy wisdom. The cooking is plain, the food plentiful and included for the help and customer alike. There is a warm feeling about these enclaves, nesting deeply in Colorado's forests, straddling mountaintops, overlooking rivers that rush and splash. The lodges are usually built of the pine or spruce woods and the stone rock of the region. The windows will surely look out upon pretty scenes.

The cowboys at these ranches often prepare breakfast for the guests on a hillside. At one well-known vacation center, the head wrangler teaches riding to first-timers and gives equestrian advice to others. Cowboys usually lead the various outings.

Meet Leslie (Les), a typical Colorado cowboy who owns one characteristic dude ranch west of Denver. Les employs a cook who feeds the guests, a clerk who checks them in, a lodge manager who looks after details. Les himself is mostly involved with the horses. His life has always evolved around animals.

He hates to wear suits, and he hates to go to the city (where he keeps an apartment all the same). He doesn't like fancy talk or talk, period. He likes horses and dogs better than people, yet at this moment he leads a group of people—experienced riders all—on another daily excursion, his second one today. He is not outgoing, yet he coddles and protects his "dudes," and no lives were ever jeopardized out here.

Les loves horses more than anything. At dawn Les had walked over to the red barn and the corral. He'd whistled. His mare, Frosty, came right out. Animal and man were one as Les rode up with the early risers, some of them very slow, typical tourists, at first fearful and uncertain. As always, two other helpers galloped ahead of the group to fry the eggs and get the pancakes ready on the griddle. The coffee boils and sends up whiffs of flavor.

Some cowboys certainly show an adaptable spirit. A few of them, for instance, also take their guests hunting for wild game in the higher mountain ranges. At one horse center, Colorado's famous luxurious C Lazy U Ranch, two of the cowboys adjusted to the times and to fads: They learned to cross-country ski and now take the guests on ski trips in winter.

Some wranglers don't work at these ranches; they're independent and merely operate their own stables on a busy highway, looking for other work in winter.

Inspired by western cowpokes, a whole industry has sprung up in the United States. Much of the fashion in jeans, denim jackets, and cowboy boots harks back to the Old West. (At the dude ranches, meanwhile, the city dwellers arrive garbed in western wear with large western hats.)

Colorado's "cowboy artists," while no longer on horseback or herding cattle, drive jeeps into the wilderness with their easels and paints. Art galleries in Denver sell the artists' output—sceneries with wild buffalo and paintings of wild horses, high mountains, and western prairies.

Colorado's cowboys are featured in American filter-cigarette ads. And cowboys even brought on a special kind of country music, which is now especially popular in America's South. Several museums around the United States exhibit cowboy gear, including saddles and spurs, as if these items were rare treasures.

Cowboy poets enjoy popularity, too. Their output can be read in newspapers; national magazines and even book publishers print their verse. Poems hang framed on dude ranch walls. The message can be brief and wise, as this little cowboy item from an anonymous author: "Never was there a cowboy who couldn't be throwed, never a bronc who couldn't be rode."

Most of the rhymes are simple, basic, perhaps a little primitive. Example? At one western ranch, a wrangler dug deeply to express the horsey West in a poem:

> *May Your Horse Never Stumble*
> *May Your Cinch Never Break*
> *May Your Belly Never Grumble*
> *May Your Heart Never Ache.*

The poem speaks a universal language.

Still a special person, the Colorado cowboy rides on.

Just south of Wolf Creek Pass on US160 lies ◆ **Pagosa Springs.** Named for the Ute word *Pahgosa,* meaning "boiling water," Pagosa Springs has a ready supply of natural geothermal energy. The main downtown area is heated with a system utilizing the naturally hot water. Near the visitors center an outdoor public hot springs offers several tubs of varying temperature for soaking cares away. The fee is a few dollars. Like any town with a natural hot springs, Pagosa claims this is the hottest natural springs in the state.

But it actually is mineral water, full of particulates and carrying a slight sulphur odor. The main hot water pool is a smelly pond enclosed by a chain-link fence, closed to the public. You wouldn't want to bathe in that one, anyway. Along the river the hot water runs through the rocks lining the edge, forming small pools of heat.

Another water wonder near Pagosa is ◆ **Treasure Falls.** This is the longest waterfall in the entire San Juan National Forest. To get there follow US160 12 miles toward the Wolf Creek summit; enjoy the magnificent alpine scenery en route. A parking area for the falls provides a safe place to leave the car away from the road. A short ¼-mile well-worn trail takes you to Colorado's miniversion of Niagara.

A *man*-made wonder close to Pagosa is ◆ **Chimney Rock.** These stone ruins were home to 2,000 Anasazi Indians more than 1,000 years ago. Still intact, these ruins are well preserved and protected. A locked gate 3 miles from the ruins prevents anyone from exploring without a National Forest Service guide. For a modest fee you can accompany the guides on their daily visits. Rock house ruins built into the hillside and the round ceremonial underground structures called kivas make the place seem as if the inhabitants just left, cleaning up before they went. Named for its towering twin spires of natural stone, Chimney Rock has been compared to Machu Picchu because it nestles in the high mountains and has grand vistas from almost every vantage point. Scholars have also suggested that during the occupation of Chimney Rock, the inhabitants were all men and that Chimney Rock was a sacred site for prayer and making powerful medicine. Contact Pagosa Springs Chamber of Commerce, P.O. Box 787, Pagosa Springs 81147; (303) 264–2360 or (800) 252–2204.

On the edge of the Pagosa Springs community there awaits a pleasant resort with accommodations, jeep tours, hikes, and even tennis and mountain biking. A large children's playground and an observation tower beckon, too. For more information: Fairfield Pagosa Resort, Box 222, Pagosa Springs 81147; (303) 731–4081.

Dramatic triangular rocks on one side; wooded mountains on the other. In between, an undulating eighteen-hole golf course, where elk congregate at dawn under ponderosa pine. Townhouses and a stately, perfectly blending lodge on a 200-foot cliff.

There is room for 850 people here, yet the year-round (deluxe) ❖**Tamarron Resort** remains a secret even to many Denverites. This remote paradise has everything—nature, atmosphere, amenities. The charming, friendly town of Durango is just 18 miles to the south. To the north of Tamarron, you see Colorado's most magnificent Alpine scenery and such legendary communities as Ouray and Silverton. Not far from the five-star resort, the Mesa Verde National Park awaits the visitor.

Built at $50 million, Tamarron was always a special oasis for the discriminating traveler. You might call it a little remote. But self-sufficiency and beauty make up for it. You would not easily forget the high-beamed rustic main lodge, plus the secluded, elegant condos that nest among hillocks and forests of aspen and fir. (The average altitude: 7,300 feet.) As you begin to size up the 620-acre grounds, you soon realize that for once, you're truly away from it all, safe and secure. The air is pure, the all-season sports on the quiet side. You can take indoor tennis lessons or cross-country ski lessons. Privacy! Downhill skiing is only minutes away at challenging Purgatory. A nonskiing visitor enjoys

113

sledding, the sleigh rides, an outing on snowshoes. All comers praise the staffed health club and masseurs.

The complex offers several dining places, fashionable shops, children's areas, Ping-Pong, wonderful jeeping, hiking, archery, and volleyball facilities. Tamarron's overall ambiance is utterly relaxed, restful, unhurried, and unworried.

The prizewinning resort opened in 1974. The lodge features an unusual swimming pool, where you can swim indoors and outdoors. There's skeet and trap shooting. Horseback expeditions depart each day from the stables, bringing you into the one-million-acre ◆ **San Juan National Forest.** Guides who are well versed in the history and ecology of the area accompany the riders through the virgin wilderness.

For the adventurous, Tamarron offers a myriad of active outdoor possibilities. For instance, the sports deck can arrange a river-rafting trip. Fishing trips are popular. Durango beckons with a historic narrow-gauge railroad, which winds its way over narrow mountain passes. The resort has its own jeeps for high country tours where you can visit old mines and wander among some fifty species of wildflowers.

Tamarron itself has many classic features. Rough-hewn beams enhance the architecture. Large, old-fashioned fireplaces make you feel comfortable. Mountain views greet you through the windows of all the restaurants and handsome convention rooms. (In summer top executives of such companies as Quaker Oats, Polaroid, and Aetna meet here.) The staff of 400 is courteous.

Bill Sageser, longtime manager of the luxury retreat, sums it up this way: "We want guests to have a pleasant experience. We want them to have fond memories."

Tamarron, the remote one, certainly succeeds. The beauty of the Colorado setting does its share, of course.

Tamarron is located 18 miles north of Durango. Fly to Durango from Denver, Albuquerque, or Phoenix. Or drive via US550 and the Navajo Trail, US160. Write Tamarron Resort, P.O. Drawer 3131, Durango 81302, or phone (800) 678–1000 nationwide, (800) 525–6493 in Colorado, or (303) 259–2000.

The bright orange cars of the ◆ **Durango-Silverton Narrow Gauge Train** seem anxious to go, as the engine chugs away waiting for passengers to board. These are original coaches and steam engines, in service since 1882. The popular tourist

114

attraction is America's last regularly scheduled narrow-gauge passenger train.

Once serving the miners and ranchers of Silverton and Durango, it now caters to passengers who want to spend three and a half hours each way thundering through spectacular mountain valleys. The excursion starts in Durango, which Will Rogers described as "out of the way and glad of it." But many people come here to experience a real western town in touch with today's world.

Fort Lewis College attracts international students for its academic standards and natural setting; this school specializes in geology studies. Durango also has the highest per capita amount of professional mountain-bike racers in the country.

On Memorial Day Weekend these athletes compete in off-road races while their compatriots, road-bike racers, line up to face an unusual competitor: the train. Yes, every year the Iron Horse Classic pits some of the country's best cyclists against the Durango-Silverton Narrow Gauge for a race from the depot in downtown Durango to Silverton, almost 50 miles away. A tribute to human endurance, bicycle racers always beat the train. But then, they aren't pulling heavy loads of eager sightseers.

Be prepared for some dust and soot. Dress accordingly.

Train reservations are required. Call the passenger agent at (303) 247–2733 or the Durango Chamber Resort Association (111 South Camino Del Rio, Durango 81302) at (303) 247–0312 or (800) 525–8855.

The admirers of this popular state speak well about Colorado's ❖**Mesa Verde National Park.** It is a ten-hour drive southwest of Denver and is about an hour west of Durango on US160, midway between Mancos and Cortez. Some 600,000 visitors come here per year.

Mesa Verde yields an extraordinary educational experience. A very small area here provides you with much that is of archaeological interest. Before you drive the distance, however, you should keep in mind that Mesa Verde differs substantially from other parks. There is no fishing here; nor is there boating, swimming, or rock climbing. Your pets have to be on a leash and are not allowed in the ruins. And you can see the historic wondrous Cliff Dwellings only in the company of park rangers.

The 21-mile road from the park entrance curves and swings

and rotates upward; its width doesn't approximate that of an interstate highway. You may have trouble if you come in a truck or try to pull a large camper. But Morefield Village campground, with its 477 camping sites, has plenty of room to park the largest RV. A separate area solely for tents provides those campers with privacy from RV generator noises. Screened with scrub oak, a small community center has a gas station, showers, Laundromat, grocery and general store, and a restaurant.

A visit to Mesa Verde National Park should be planned with care. Earmark one or two days for the park itself and try to arrive early in the day or during the off-season. The historical scene and the colors come through especially well if you can visit Mesa Verde at dawn. The moment you see the sudden, flat-topped

Cliff Palace, Mesa Verde National Park

plateau, the cliff dwellings of a prehistoric civilization, you'll be happy that you braved the distance. No other national park can equal this one.

Begin with a visit to the park museum for clues to the mysterious Basket Weavers. These Indians left behind an amazing array of agricultural tools, pottery, and baskets. The tribes arrived in the area around A.D. 450 and abandoned the site in 1276. It took another 500 years for Spanish explorers to discover the old, russet blocks of stone, the turrets and primitive apartments known as cliff dwellings hanging under a canopy of glorious rock. You will never forget the Balcony House and Cliff Palace.

At its height the Mesa Verde Plateau supported 50,000 Indians. By the close of the thirteenth century, it was completely deserted. What happened to the Anasazi is not known, but archaeologists theorize that a thirty-year drought starting in 1246, combined with soil that had been depleted by constant use, caused successive crop failures and that the Anasazi moved farther south into New Mexico and Arizona.

The National Park Service does a good job of looking after Mesa Verde's 80-mile area of ponderosa pine, spruce trees, and juniper, all laced by a few paths. Not a billboard or soft-drink sign in sight.

When visiting Mesa Verde you're not too far from the Four Corners area of Colorado, Utah, New Mexico, and Arizona. This is butte country. The sky is even bluer here in the southwestern corner of the state. The plains seem to stretch wider than in the northern corners. The Colorado peaks resemble those of the Alps, with jutting slopes and deeply carved valleys. (Bring a warm change of clothes.) The people are easygoing and glad to see you come.

After the Mesa Verde experience, your own state or province will never be the same again. For information: Mesa Verde National Park 81330; (303) 529–4461 or 529–4421.

A 50-mile drive from the historic canyons of Mesa Verde will take you to another area of Indian ruins. This is little-known ◆**Hovenweep National Monument,** west of Cortez, Colorado, on gravel and rough blacktop roads. You will escape the crowds when you visit these ruins.

Here the terrain is high desert plateau. Sagebrush and scattered juniper trees dot the horizon. It seems desolate, almost barren. But there was life here. A canyon opens in the plateau, and scattered cottonwood trees indicate the presence of water. A spring still flows into a small depression in the shadow of the canyon wall. This water was the center of the community 700 years ago. The towers of Hovenweep are thought to be watch towers and fortifications to protect this precious liquid resource.

With artistic skill that would rival a stone mason's today, ancient Pueblo Indians built these towers in several configurations. Round, square, and oval structures dot the canyon edge. Each rock was trimmed to fit exactly with its neighbor, and the lines of the buildings are straight and almost smooth. Small peepholes and keyhole entrances could have provided views of a possible enemy approaching or just been a way to keep an eye on the rest of the community. Standing at the structure called Hovenweep Castle, you can look east and see a tower on almost every promontory of the canyon. Hiking and interpretive trails link most of these. Allow at least a half-day to explore the exposed ruins.

The ranger station is open year-round and has a great bookstore, small museum, water, and a soda-pop machine. Don't count on buying lunch here, because Hovenweep has no food concession. A quiet little campground with picnic tables and water beckons, however. Small fee for camping; no fee to hike around Hovenweep. For information: Superintendent, Hovenweep National Monument, McElmo Route, Cortez 81321; (303) 529–4461 or 529–4465.

The Ute Indians are the oldest continuous residents of Colorado of the seven original tribes who still live in the southwestern part of the state today. For those with an interest in Native American culture, the city of Durango is the gateway to both the
◆ **Southern Ute and Mountain Ute Reservations.**
Nearly a century ago these Indians accepted government allotments and settled on a strip of land along the Colorado–New Mexico border, near the present town of Ignacio (population 667). Eventually these Utes became known as the Southern Ute Indian tribe. Claiming more than 1,000 members, the Utes have their headquarters in Ignacio.

Here they have built an Indian Country vacation complex, complete with a thirty-eight-room motel, indoor/outdoor pool, museum, and a fine arts and crafts shop. The tribe lives on a reservation.

The present-day Utes can hardly be distinguished from any other Americans. Sounds of their television sets, radios, and VCRs fill their modern-day urban homes. Basketball and swimming are popular reservation sports. Many Utes drive to the nearest towns for shopping, movies, and restaurants.

Luckily, their society does allow the dynamic combination of both traditional and modern cultures. Depending upon age, education, job, and values, some of these Native Americans continue to speak the Ute language. They handmake their clothes and do traditional work in arts and crafts. Others prefer to live the modern American life. The tribe itself and the Bureau of Indian Affairs employ most of the Utes today.

The ancestral home of these Native Americans once spanned most of the present state of Colorado. Although reigning over a large empire, they lacked a common Ute political organization. Instead, they formed independent bands, which followed their own chiefs. The most famous groups included the Uncompahgre or Tabeguache, whose central home was the area around the present sites of Gunnison and Montrose, Colorado; the White River and Yampa bands of northwestern Colorado; the Mouache, who roamed along the front range of the Rockies in Colorado; the Capotes, who lived in the San Luis Valley of Colorado; and the Weminuche, who lived in the San Juan Basin in southwestern Colorado.

While hunting and roaming their enormous territory, the Utes often fought against other tribes, yet they remained on generally good terms with white men who trapped, traded, and prospected for gold on Indian lands.

As Anglo settlers streamed onto Colorado's eastern slope, the government, fearing trouble between Anglos and Utes, tried to persuade the Utes to move to the west of the Continental Divide. Finding it difficult to negotiate with so many chiefs, the government designated an Uncompahgre leader, Ouray—his name meant "arrow"—as the Ute tribal spokesman. Chief Ouray wanted to preserve his home and Ute territory; he resisted departure from the San Luis Valley and surrounding areas. Finally, under the treaty of 1868, the Native Americans agreed to move westward.

Subsequent treaties and promises made and broken resulted in combative Indians. Trouble erupted when Utes attacked and killed U.S. soldiers in the Meeker and Thornburgh massacres, and they were later driven off their lands.

These days all is peaceful in southern Colorado, though, and the Native Americans welcome tourists, especially since legalized

119

gambling is allowed on the reservation. Glitzy casinos offer several types of gaming and bingo.

The Southern Ute Indian Reservation is connected with the Southern Ute Agency of the Bureau of Indian Affairs, Ignacio 81137.

For the visitor the cultural center (719–563–4525) is of special interest. You reach Ignacio via SR172 from Durango.

Sand dunes in Colorado? What a surprise! Geologists say that the sand stretches such as those of the ❖ **Great Sand Dunes National Monument** are usually the handiwork of the world's oceans. Didn't the salt water have millions of years to crush, mash, and pulverize the land? The sea pushed, licked, and retreated, eroding rocks into small particles and grinding earth to fine silt. Moreover, winds blew sand grains from the mountains to our plains. The source of sand is sediments, eroded in time by winds and glaciers, washed into the dunes. More recently, the drying southwesterly winds carried the sands into what is today the Great Sand Dunes National Monument. Erosive forces and more winds helped fashion sand peaks that crest to 600 feet above the valley floor.

The Great Sand Dunes National Monument looks as if it had been lifted from Africa's Kalahari Desert. White men didn't discover these dunes until 1599, when the Spanish explorers crossed the sands.

According to Colorado historian Richard Grant, pictures taken in 1927 show that the main dunes have undergone very little change in the past fifty years. Except that in 1932 they became a national monument—the Great Sand Dunes.

The monument takes in about 46,000 acres of this ocean of sand. Although there are many activities available, hiking on the dunes is everyone's first choice. Visitors can go anywhere they want. It's best to take off your shoes and wade across the soft, water-cooled sand creek, but be sure to wear shoes into the dunes. In midsummer the sand can get as hot as 140°F.

On the other side of the stream, the dunes are incredibly massive—some rising seventy stories above the valley floor—and, due to shadows, deceptively steep. The valley floor is 7,500 feet above sea level, making breathing difficult at first for those not adjusted to the altitude.

But there are few experiences that can compare with being on the dunes. It is like riding in the frozen waves of a storm-blown sea. You climb to the top of a ridge, taking in a view of the gold and tan waves stretching for miles to the towering blue mountains, then descend the trough until you are in a valley completely surrounded by immense hills of sand. These are America's tallest sand dunes, rising to 700 feet. The highest dune is located opposite the visitor center, and it takes about three hours to hike to the top and return. From the top you can see nearly the entire area, as well as a large segment of Colorado's Sangre de Cristo Range.

Great Sand Dunes National Monument is located on SR17 in the south central part of the state, just a few miles off US160, the main east-west highway through southern Colorado. SR17 is a scenic north-south alternative route to I–25.

Admission is $1.00 per car. Pinyon Flats campground in the monument is open May to October. Great Sand Dunes National Monument, Mosca 81146; (719) 378–2312.

DENVER AND THE PLAINS

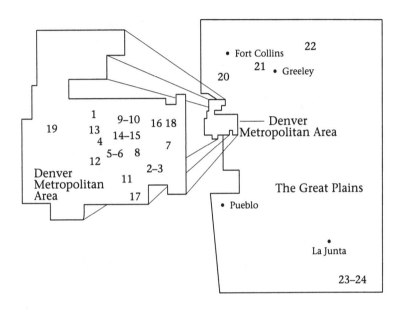

- Fort Collins
22
20
21 • Greeley

1
9–10 16 18
19
13 14–15
4 7
12 5–6 8
2–3
Denver
Metropolitan 11
Area 17

Denver
Metropolitan Area

The Great Plains

• Pueblo

•
La Junta

23–24

1. Oxford Hotel
2. Molly Brown House
3. Governor's Mansion
4. Westin Center
5. Denver Center Theatre
6. Boettcher Concert Hall
7. Normandy
8. Duffy's Shamrock Inn
9. National Western Stock Show and Rodeo
10. Denver Coliseum
11. Buckhorn Exchange
12. Forney Historical Transportation Museum
13. Larimer Square
14. Museum of Western Art
15. Brown Palace Hotel
16. Queen Anne Inn
17. Wellshire Inn
18. Washington Park
19. Sloan's Lake
20. Loveland
21. Centennial Village
22. Pawnee Buttes
23. Bent's Old Fort
24. Picketwire Canyon

DENVER AND THE PLAINS

DENVER METROPOLITAN AREA

There were the Spaniards and the Native American tribes—Utes, Cheyennes, Arapahos, and Cherokees. Then suddenly came the prospectors to that prairie wilderness 10 miles east of the mountain ramparts. The fate of a tranquil Native American village at the junction of Cherry Creek and South Platte River would be changed forever.

That summer day in 1858, the Anglo visitors found gold in these waters.

Word of the find soon spread. "The New Eldorado!" shouted the midwestern papers. That spring an estimated 150,000 people began to trek across the wide plains aboard wagons and even on foot. Only 40,000 made it or stayed; others turned back.

Gold in paying quantities was far from common. Those first months were very hard. Yet that year a people's court was organized. The first hotel—The Denver House—opened. Publisher William N. Byers reached Denver on April 21, 1859, with a printing outfit. On April 23 he issued the first newspaper printed in Colorado. William McGaa was the first child born in Denver. Leavenworth and Pikes Peak Express ran the first stage to Denver. The Auraria Post Office was established.

That May John H. Gregory discovered a vein of gold-bearing quartz near what was to become Central City. This was big news, and, at first, it nearly evacuated Denver. As mines were developed in the mountains, however, Denver grew in her coming role as an important trade center. Indeed, Horace Greeley suggested, "Go West, young man! Go West, young man!" Denver became the logical jumping-off point for the huge gold finds of Central City and Black Hawk.

Exaggerated accounts of the discovery traveled eastward, causing the Gold Rush of 1859. Thousands of fortune hunters hurried across the plains, on foot, on horseback, in wagons, some even pushing handcarts and wheelbarrows. Most of these failed to find the mineral and trudged wearily back home. But they had founded several little habitation clusters variously known as Auraria and Denver City (named after General James W. Denver, territorial governor of Kansas), and these gradually became the capital city of Colorado.

All through the late 1850s and early 1860s, a great mass of people surged back and forth in search of wealth. Conditions were primitive in these Colorado camps. Tents were eventually replaced by huts, which grew into shacks, log cabins, and finally houses.

Gold brought more fortune hunters from all over North America but also Irish engineers, Welsh hard-rock miners, and other Europeans, 100,000 more people in all. For a period between the 1870s and 1890s, Colorado had so many Germans that the laws were printed in both German and English.

Lots of problems and calamities awaited the city.

Early in 1863 a great fire destroyed much of the business district. The following summer the lush plains were scorched by a drought. The winter was cold beyond all previous experience. Then in the spring of 1864, a flash flood churned along the Cherry Creek sand bed through the city, washing over houses and bridges and killing twenty persons. Nearly $1 million worth of property was destroyed.

In the wake of these natural disasters, the Indians attacked. Stage stations were sacked, communication and supply lines to the East severed. Denver was left with only a week's supply of food.

But the city survived, and because of the hardships the local people developed a determination to keep on surviving. When the Union Pacific Railroad bypassed Colorado on its transcontinental route, Denver citizens raised $300,000 and built their *own* railroad to meet the Union Pacific at Cheyenne, Wyoming.

Soon the Kansas Pacific crossed the plains. According to historian Richard Grant, "The silver barons built elaborate mansions on Capitol Hill. Gamblers, drifters and gunmen flooded the saloons and gaming halls on Larimer and Market streets. Bat Masterson tended bar here, Soapy Smith ran the West's largest gang of thieves, crooks and con artists, and anyone who was anyone in the 'Old West' paid at least a visit to Denver's mud-filled, honky-tonk streets."

On August 1, 1876, Colorado entered the Union and was called the Centennial State in honor of the one hundredth anniversary of the Declaration of Independence.

By 1879 The Mile High City had a population of 35,000 and boasted the first telephone service in the West. Soon there was a second boom. One silver mining camp after another suddenly prospered. When the silver played out, Denver settled into a comfortable, respectable life—nearly free of gamblers, drifters, and claim jumpers.

Education now became important. In 1887 Governor Ben H. Eaton told the General Assembly: "The schools of Denver are today equal to the best in the world—equal to those of Boston, Paris or Berlin. The capital of our state is the Athens of the plains, with the glory of ancient Athens."

By 1910 the city had become the commercial and industrial center of the Rocky Mountain region, with a large cattle market and the largest sheep market in the world. Denver was in the process of becoming the nation's second capital, thanks to a proliferation of government offices. This situation is still true today; Denver is second only to Washington, D.C., in number of employed government workers.

Many older Denverites still harbor a nostalgic feeling about Colorado Victoriana, and some people are seriously trying to hold onto the city's remaining old mansions. There is public resistance to the wreckers sent by those who prefer the profit of more office buildings and highrise apartment houses. Many of the noted old edifices, the Tabor Theater and the Windsor Hotel among them, had to give way to the modern glass and steel skyscrapers. "Part of Denver died tonight," said a Denverite the day another of the historic hotels was razed.

A few of the Victorian homes still exist, complete with the cherrywood dressers and mantelpieces, hat racks and cherrywood mirror frames. The Brown Palace and the ✦Oxford Hotel still stand. While in the city, you may wish to visit one of the old mansions, such as the ✦Molly Brown House, where history is preserved.

After she became wealthy, the "Unsinkable" Molly Brown lived her flamboyant life in this mansion of native Colorado lavastone. Following Molly's death in 1932, the building served as a roominghouse. Then at the whim of each new owner, it was remodeled or divided. Rescued in 1971 by "Historic Denver," the mansion was decorated as Molly herself had done, using old photographs Molly had taken of her home's interior. The Molly Brown House has been restored to its exaggerated, extreme opulence. It is located at 1340 Pennsylvania Street, Denver 80218;

(303) 832–4092. Summer tour hours, June through August, are 10:00 A.M. to 4:00 P.M., Monday through Friday. Winter tour hours, September through May, are 10:00 A.M. to 3:30 P.M., Tuesday through Saturday, and noon to 3:30 P.M. Sunday. Small fee.

Colorado's ◆ **Governor's Mansion,** a red brick Colonial building with white stone trim, was built by one of the state's distinguished pioneer families, the Cheesmans. Cheesman Park is named for them. After serving as the home of John Evans, Colorado's second territorial governor, the property passed into the Boettcher family. Then it became part of their Boettcher Foundation, a philanthropic organization that presented it as a gift to the state of Colorado in 1960. The mansion has been the executive residence of the state's governors ever since.

Furnished with luxurious art, antiques, and furniture, the house is available for limited tours. It is located at 400 East Eighth Avenue; tours are conducted free on Tuesday afternoons, from 1:00 to 3:00 P.M., May through August. Contact the Colorado Historical Society, 1300 Broadway, Denver 80203; (303) 866–3682.

Even in these transient times, most Denverites refuse to relocate to another city. "Move?" says one executive. "They offered me a promotion on the East Coast. But I refused. Stayed on at a lower salary." If you ask longtime Denver people why they're so partial to their city, you'll get a long string of explanations. "We ski. The mountains are close." "We love the many parks and green lawns of the homes." "Do you know a more cosmopolitan place between Los Angeles and Chicago? Denver is *it!*"

The denizens of the Colorado state capital mention the educational and cultural possibilities, the libraries and workshops and seminars, the geographically central location, the generally low unemployment rate, and the beautification of the city during the past decades, what with Larimer Square, the Tivoli Complex, the ◆ **Westin Center,** the Sixteenth Street Mall, and the superelegant Cherry Creek Shopping Complex.

Because the mountains are only thirty minutes away from downtown, Denver attracts a young, energetic population. This dynamic energy is reflected in Denver's nightlife. The city boasts more than 2,000 restaurants, more than 100 art galleries, almost 30 theaters, 100 cinemas, an $80 million performing arts center, a new convention center, and dozens of nightclubs, discos, comedy clubs, singles bars, and concert halls.

127

Denver leads the nation in movie attendance per capita, is in the top five cities for book purchases, and is a growing center for jazz. But if there is one thing Denver does well (after 130 years of practice), it is the saloon. The first permanent structure in Denver was a saloon, and today there are sports bars, art bars, fern bars, outdoor cafe bars, English pubs, "Old West" saloons, rock bars, city-overlook bars, country and western bars, art deco bars, and even bars that don't serve alcohol. (Denver leads the nation in beer brewing, however.)

And the legendary climate! Denverites enjoy recreation all year; many outdoor swimming pools are open throughout the four seasons. The Rocky Mountains screen the city from temperature extremes. Spring temperatures are pleasant. When much of the United States swelters in the summer heat, the mountains' air conditioning keeps Denverites reasonably cool. It seldom rains. Mean precipitation is only 14 inches annually. Unceasing day-after-day torrents are unknown. (Showers usually last just minutes.) Late autumn—even October and November—can bring exceptionally beautiful weather that the natives call Indian Summer. Winters are mild. The dry mountain air is invigorating but never extreme. (On occasion, however, temperature inversions and lack of wind make for too much air pollution.)

The climate encourages outdoor pursuits. As a result, Denver has more sporting goods stores and ski shops per capita than most any other population center in the world and a corresponding number of recreation facilities that include free tennis courts, city golf courses, and the like.

At the same time, filmmakers, artists, and thinkers all gravitate toward Denver, a city that spent $6 million to build an art museum. The main public library, with its 1.2 million volumes, happens to be one of the best—and most versatile—in the West. It is at the library desks that you get the feeling of Denver's wide horizons.

Denver's genuine penchant for culture shows up in several ways. On a given evening the visitor to the state capital could take in a play by Dylan Thomas at the boldly designed ❖ **Denver Center Theatre.** Next door, in the futuristic 2,700-seat ❖ **Boettcher Concert Hall,** the music lovers can enjoy the artistry of duo-pianists from Italy, an Israeli violinist, the top singers from the Metropolitan or the Colorado Symphony, and

128

Denver Art Museum

the 110-member Colorado choir, plus soloists, excelling in Handel's *Messiah*. The city has come of age culturally, what with its little theaters, its art cinemas, its ballets, and its chamber music ensembles. Art galleries beckon by the dozen, and it is not unusual to come upon traveling exhibits from Mexico, Spain, Belgium, and other countries.

Local interest is keen in the rest of the world. And Denver's citizens remain helpful and hospitable, especially toward tourists and guests. Just tell a Denverite that you arrived here yesterday from London or Frankfurt or Minneapolis or wherever. Doors will spring wide open. Denverites will show off their clean city; they may want to take you to their homes, where the inevitable sprinklers deepen the green of the lawns and flower gardens.

Denver arouses special interest because of its ethnic variety. The Hispanic population is fascinating for its rich and proud heritage.

In north Denver you find the classic Italian grocery stores that sell prosciutto, salami, black olives, and *tonno* as do those in Italy.

Genuine Italian restaurants serve you homemade pasta and black olives and you drink Chianti, just as you would in Naples, Salerno, or Parma.

There is a Polish club in Denver, where the young Polish girls still wear the pretty national costumes for their national folk dances.

A small Denver contingent is German speaking, with a lasting interest in dancing *schuhplattler* and singing all the old songs. The Germans founded an appropriately named Edelweiss Club, a Goethe Club, and the *Turnverein*, where the men actually do strenuous calisthenics and play soccer on weekends. Denver has its own German/Swiss *Delikatessen* stores, which import marinated herring from Kiel and Hamburg, Westphalian hams, and landjaeger sausages and sell their customers Nivea suntan creams, German Oldo toothpaste, and *Der Stern* magazine, much as in Manhattan's Yorkville area.

There is a sizable Japanese population, with its own stores and customs, and a Buddhist Temple for weddings. Vietnamese immigrants have their own shopping centers, and you will find Korean shops.

There is also Denver's enthusiasm for international dining. Well-traveled, polyglot restaurateurs like Pierre Wolfe often appear on television or radio. Heinz Gerstle, another foreign cuisine expert, has founded a local gourmet club. It should come as no surprise that the city has a number of authentic (and expensive) French eating places (among others, the ◆**Normandy,** La Coupole, Mont Petit, Le Central). Denver's dozens of superb oriental restaurants include the well-regarded Mandarin and Szechuan La Chine (expensive). The visitor can also dine on genuine Ethiopian, Afghan, Moroccan, Greek, Armenian, Hungarian, Swiss, German, Italian, and, of course, Mexican fare. How about the traveler from the British Isles? On Denver's west side the Wuthering Heights restaurant displays medieval armor and enriches its longish menu with Prime English steak, Filet of Beef Wellington, and an English boneless chicken breast (expensive). At the foot of the new downtown skyscrapers, meanwhile, ◆**Duffy's Shamrock Inn** holds court with (inexpensive) Irish home cooking, followed by real Irish coffee. This pub serves a filling supper at a reasonable price (1635 Court Place; 303–534–4953).

To be sure, the city's better restaurants, its bistros and more worldly nightspots, and its extra-elegant central hotels are accustomed to and welcome the visitor from abroad.

Usually Denverites show off the Museum of Western Art or the elegant western history department of the Main Library or the cowboy statues at the Civic Center.

You might trust their touristic judgment, what with Denver and environs attracting more than ten million visitors a year. "Smile!" goes one of the state's slogans, "You live in Colorado!" And most Denverites smile a lot as they count their blessings.

Denver Metro Convention and Visitor Bureau, 225 West Colfax, Denver 80202; (303) 892–1505 or (800) 265–6723.

Of all the year-round events that take place in Denver, this one, by golly, is the biggest, longest, and most original—a yearly happening that radiates authenticity, excitement, and entertainment. Yup, it's the ◆ **National Western Stock Show and Rodeo.** Sixty years ago cowboys' competitions with one another were formalized into rodeos. The stock show was born in a circus tent in 1906; the high speed of the riders, the antics of the rodeo clowns, and the sweet smells of the animals sometimes still remind you of a circus. For approximately two weeks every January, old Buffalo Bill and his Wild West entertainers seem to return to old Denver Town.

The National Western remains an important stock show, too. You can view more than 15,000 live, scrubbed, and brushed Herefords, Angus, Simmentals, Shorthorns, Longhorns, Arabian horses, Morgan horses, draft horses, miniature horses, ewes, and lambs, all in their neat pens. You watch shearing contests, breeding cattle auctions, and the judging of quarterhorse stallions. Some 500,000 visitors flock to the arenas to buy, sell, learn, and socialize. Millions of dollars exchange hands here.

"This is a cowboy convention for real-life cowboys," says one longtime Stock Show regular. "It's big business for the people who grow the stuff that ends up in our refrigerators and stomachs."

In addition to the judging and auctions, there are lectures, sales booths, meetings, and contests for the cattlemen and -women who show up here. Lots of money is in evidence. Thousand-dollar alligator boots. Hundred-dollar Stetsons. Belt buckles with diamonds. Even silver halters for the horses. A big commerce in livestock supplies, raw wool, saddles, cow tags, western art show and sale, lassoes.

131

New techniques are taught in feeding and breeding. In the arenas you see riding demonstrations by horsewomen who gallop at a breakneck pace. Red-vested auctioneers and a peopled tribune asplash in color pay attention to a sale of—yes!—*llamas*. A children's area delights the young ones with displays of baby rabbits, geese, and piglets. Each weekday some 1,200 schoolchildren are bused here to see the animals. The multifaceted spectacular not only brings aristocratic purebred livestock to Denver. The Stock Show regularly attracts the best of the rodeo ring, all top contenders for national championships for female barrel racing, calf roping, bull and bronco riding, steer wrestling, and many more events by more than 1,000 professional rodeo cowboys and cowgirls who are courageous and sporty. More than $400,000 in prizes are at stake.

But not all cowboys do well in Denver. A horse may refuse to buck and the rider will get nothing. A horse tosses him off after two seconds and the rider will get nothing. "They're the great American gamblers on horseback," says a western radio announcer.

Rodeo riders may be among the last American heroes or heroines. It takes nerve to tackle a furious, crowd-crazed animal and stay on it for eight seconds. It takes true guts to look injury in the eye without flinching.

Nobody gives the competitors an expense account. They pay their own way to ride at the National Western Stock Show. The rodeo cowboy draws no allowance, has no guaranteed annual wage. The only income comes from earnings in a fiercely competitive sport where he must win not only against other men but against the "rank" (mean) animals. And he must pay for this privilege—entry fees that can run into several hundred dollars per event per rodeo.

Most riders hail from small towns and made their first acquaintance with horses as kids. One typical bareback champ comes from Cora, Wyoming. He started as a ranch hand.

Rodeos, such as the National Western in Denver, may have well begun as a prank, a diversion for ranch hands, cowpokes. A few specialists, the "roughstring" riders who busted wild horses for a livelihood at $3.00 to $5.00 apiece, were quick to show their stuff. They were a tough bunch of men. Hardened by the summer heat and winter blizzards, used to riding through long nights, they had to deal with stampeding herds, crippled animals, and cattle rustlers. Their horses were extensions of themselves. They lived in the saddle.

Rodeo must have started during the early cattle drives and on the scattered ranches. A historian of the Denver-based Professional Rodeo Cowboys Association explains: "When their work was done, the cowboys entertained each other with roping and riding contests, showing off the skills they had sharpened during their everyday work on the range."

In the early 1880s American ranchers began to develop the "ranch show" as a spectator sport. Already in 1888 Colorado spectators paid money to watch cowboys on bucking broncs. Within twenty years these affairs had become known as rodeos and were drawing crowds on tour in the cities of the United States.

In the early days of rodeo, the rider stayed in the saddle "until the horse was rode or the cowboy throwed." Today the saddle bronc rider must stay aboard eight seconds while at the same time not disqualifying himself in any number of ways. A man has to zoom out of the chute with both feet in the stirrups.

As a spectator you can see lots of thrilling action, all the while being seated comfortably in the ◆ **Denver Coliseum.** The Stock Show grounds sprawl across 150 acres, which are only about 100 yards south of I–70. Buses get you there all day long; free shuttles run from various downtown hotels. You can also take a cab or drive. In that case, keep in mind that thousands of visiting livestock folks and rodeo fans compete for room to leave their cars, so close-in parking isn't always plentiful.

Rodeo competition takes place both afternoons and evenings. Tickets cost no more than for a movie. But wait! Have you ever been to a motion picture where you could witness a llama auction, an Australian-style sheep-shearing contest, the world's largest bull show (with one animal actually selling at $300,000), a catch-a-calf competition for teenagers? What film lets you talk to a real, true-blue Colorado rancher?

National Western Stock Show and Rodeo, 4655 Humboldt Street, Denver 80216; (303) 297–1166.

How would you like to dine in a historic landmark and museum? How about a steaming platter of elk steak at a table under a stuffed elk or a plate heaped with buffalo meat, with mounted buffalos staring down? The ◆ **Buckhorn Exchange** is allegedly Colorado's oldest restaurant (it celebrated its centennial in 1993). It is certainly one of the most original. Moreover, it's a saloon, a magnet for celebrities and tourists, and a moneymaker.

Supper here appeals to well-heeled meat eaters: twenty-four-ounce T-bone steaks, fourteen-ounce New York steaks, buffalo meat, baby back ribs, Rocky Mountain oysters, rabbit—all at hefty deluxe rates in a noisy, congenial atmosphere. The saloon is upstairs, complete with a giant oak bar that was shipped here by ox cart. Nearby walls are filled with 1902 photos of hunting parties; even the men's room has historical pictures of stagecoaches.

The downstairs restaurant-museum is cluttered with more than 500 taxidermy pieces, including antelopes, deer, bears, wolverines, mountain goats, moose, weasels, zebras, and birds of all kinds, shapes, and plumage. You can look at more than a hundred rifles, pistols, and other weapons. You dine at 110-year-old poker tables covered with cozy red-checkered tablecloths. There's lunch, too, if you want it, with good pot roast, a Buckhorn dip, bratwurst, or the specialty of the house, a navy bean soup. Lunch is popular with the downtown Yuppie business crowd; dinner attracts out-of-towners that include many Europeans. Europe can never match the Buckhorn's true-blue American West.

Even the restaurant's history has its fascinating aspects. It was begun in 1893 by owner Henry H. Zietz, a cowboy and scout with Buffalo Bill, no less; personal bodyguard of Leadville's silver millionaire H. A. W. Horace Tabor; and hunting guide of President Teddy Roosevelt, who actually arrived in his private train in front of the Buckhorn. The restaurant's official history relates that Henry Zietz "catered to cattlemen, miners, railroad builders, Indian chiefs, silver barons, roustabouts, gamblers, the great and the near-great." In December 1900 a masked gunman rode up to the restaurant, waved a .45, and demanded all money and valuables to be placed on the bar, "and be quick about it!" The fellow's horse had been tied to the Buckhorn's hitching post, but when the gunman rode away at a gallop, he found himself pursued by Zietz's rifle-raising customers, who "handily dispatched the miscreant to greener pastures."

After the Zietz family's death, the restaurant-museum passed into the capable hands of several historically minded Denver investors, who put large sums into restoring the building and its contents in 1978. They also raised the prices to twentieth-century levels. The Buckhorn is in the National Register of Historic Places by order of the Department of the Interior.

A meal here will delight Texans and other travelers from all over the world.

The Buckhorn's red brick building is easy to find at 1000 Osage Street, Denver 80204. More details? The location is between Colfax Avenue and Eight Avenue, 5 blocks west of Santa Fe Boulevard.

The Buckhorn Exchange is open for lunch (expensive) Monday through Friday from 11:30 A.M. to 2:30 P.M., and dinner is served seven nights a week, starting at 5:30 P.M. (deluxe). Reservations suggested. (303) 534–9505.

The ❖Forney Historical Transportation Museum hugs the downtown area. You reach it via Denver's network of superhighways. You can also arrive at the address by private or rental car or taxi. The museum is easy to find. It sits in all its massiveness at The Valley Highway (I–25) and Speer Boulevard (I–25 exit 211 northbound, exit 212C southbound). Here you can see some old vehicles, including 1915 Cadillacs, 1905 Fords, various old surreys, a locomobile, an ancient electric car, various carriages, bygone cycles, rail coaches, steam engines, and old airplanes. The notable exhibits include Theodore Roosevelt's Tour Car, Aly Khan's Rolls-Royce, and Amelia Earhart's Gold Bug Kissel. The children run to see the ladies' old, old dresses or the officers' military uniforms dating back to 1750 and 1800. The Forney Transportation Museum is open every day except Christmas, Thanksgiving, and New Year's Day: summer, 9:00 A.M.–5:00 P.M.; winter, 11:00 A.M.–5:00 P.M.; Sundays, 11:00 A.M.–5:30 P.M. Adults $4.00, youth $2.00, child $1.00; group rates are available.

For more information write Forney Historical Transportation Museum, 1416 Platte Street, Denver 80202; call (303) 433–3643.

❖Larimer Square is a renovated eighteenth-century downtown oasis with a national reputation; indeed, it is the second most visited landmark in Colorado. (The Air Force Academy is the first.)

In 1858 General William E. Larimer erected Denver's first building here. It was a mere log cabin. More than one hundred years later, a group of Colorado businesspeople founded the Larimer Square Association for the purpose of restoring the old buildings. The excitement that once was historic Larimer Street soon returned in the form of promenades, carriage rides, and quaint shops between Fourteenth and Fifteenth streets.

In some ways Larimer Square reminds you of Ghirardelli Square in San Francisco. Or it may make you think of Greenwich Village or New Orleans's French quarter; others compare it to Chicago's Old Town or Toronto's Yorktown. By the same token, Larimer Square has its own visual personality; it remains an outstanding example of early Denver Victorian architecture, complete with gaslights, handwrought leaded-glass windows, stairways, historic markers, restored cornices, and handsome outdoor benches for resting and watching. In the restaurants (pricey) and shops, you find Tiffany lamps, cherrywood bars, rosewood paneling, old wallpapers, and lead ceilings.

The Square is paved with the legends of the nineteenth century.

Larimer Street in Denver was once the most famous thoroughfare in the West. The restaurants, hotels, and theaters of its heyday were renowned. Stories of what happened when the greats, near-greats, and desperados of the West met made good newspaper copy. And tales of what went on behind closed doors in the neighborhood shocked a nation. Gambling and boozing were rampant.

Named for Denver's founder, General William E. Larimer, the street played a prominent role in the city's political and commercial history from November 16, 1858. That first day Denver City consisted only of Larimer Street's 1400 block. As the western town grew around it, the original site became Denver's first commercial and governmental center. Here were the first post office, the first department store, the first drugstore, and the first bank and government buildings of the 1860s, 1870s, and 1880s.

As the years passed, Denver gradually moved uptown, and Larimer Street became a skid row area. Thanks to the gin mills and flophouses, the handsome Victorian buildings were forgotten, although amid the grime and dirt, their architectural beauty remained. Razing was a frequent threat.

Larimer Square is now a Landmark Preservation District. You find this important Denver tourist attraction listed in the National Register of Historic Places.

The 2-block Larimer Street area between Fourteenth and Fifteenth streets is easily reached on foot or by free shuttle from Denver's downtown hotels. For information call (303) 534–2367.

Do you know a museum devoted exclusively to western art? Such museums are scarce indeed. And there is no better way to bring the frontier alive than through name painters—the great ones such as Albert Bierstadt, Karl Bodmer, Thomas Moran, Charles Russell, Thomas Hart Benton, Ernest Blumenschein—or through the action-packed bronze statues of Frederic Remington. These are hallowed art names—many from the last century—artists who still knew how to *draw* or paint traditional oils or watercolors (unlike some contemporaries, who are able only to splash color on a canvas or use the ruler for straight minimalist lines).

Denver's ❖**Museum of Western Art** opened in 1983. A Colorado governor spoke of it glowingly as "providing a missing link." Denverites and visitors have paid homage to the chronologically arranged art. Its themes fit perfectly into Colorado and frontier history: rousing scenes of trappers facing bears, buffalo hunts, cattle roundups, Indian fights, attacks on trains or stagecoaches, canyonlands, waterfalls, and magnificent mountains. Each canvas or watercolor reflects artistic integrity and perfect control of the medium—rare qualities indeed.

The building that houses the collection sits across from the famous Brown Palace Hotel. The museum was well designed as a mix of renovation and restoration, complete with a bookstore in the basement. One area is reserved for special exhibitions, such as Thomas Moran's well-known Yellowstone illustrations, produced on location during an 1871 expedition. The 125 or so paintings—and the existence of the Denver-based museum—all came together through the efforts of William Foxley, a Montana cattleman and entrepreneur. It was Foxley who sought out the many owners and collectors of the Remingtons, Russells, Bierstadts, and many more. The acquisition of these artworks proved to be a difficult task, as was finding a site and getting assistance from the Colorado Senate.

Even before the museum's inauguration in 1983, the Victorian building itself had an interesting history. The site at 1727 Tremont Place started as a school that taught "Christian virtues" to young ladies. After the building owner's death a few years later, the school took on a new life as Hotel Richelieu and finally the Navarre. Ironically, these were gambling and sex establishments for the nouveaux riches of the West. In 1892 an underground tunnel began to link the Navarre with the Brown

137

Palace—which became a discreet passageway to the brothel and gaming activities. In 1904 the address was turned into a fine restaurant, which continued business under various managements until 1977. William Foxley's efforts followed. The building is listed in the National Register of Historic Places.

The Museum of Western Art depends on the modest admission fee and on contributions plus memberships. The location is 1727 Tremont Place; the phone is (303) 296–1880. Visiting hours: Monday, 1:00–4:00 P.M.; Tuesday through Saturday, 10:00 A.M.–4:30 P.M.

From its international debut in 1892 until the present, Denver's ✦ **Brown Palace Hotel** has lived up to its motto, "Where the World Registers." Indeed, this historic hotel is a classic. Celebrities and royalty have graced its corridors. Katharine Hepburn, Bob Hope, Molly Brown, the Beatles, King Hussein of Jordan, and every U.S. president since Theodore Roosevelt have spent time here.

The Brown, as Denverites have nicknamed it, is a remarkable example of Victorian architecture. The hotel lobby impresses the most. Upon entering, your eyes look up the six tiers of wrought-iron balconies to the stained-glass cathedral ceiling. The decorative stone on the pillars is Mexican onyx. Changing displays of historical memorabilia decorate the luxurious lobby. Old guest registers, menus, and photographs take you back to relive the role the Brown Palace played in the history of Denver.

The hotel is named for its builder, Henry Cordes Brown. As Brown watched nineteenth-century Denver grow, he saw the need for a fine hostelry for visiting easterners who came to do business with Colorado mining companies and railroads. The builder envisioned this fine edifice to rise from a triangular plot of land he owned near the center of the city. Henry Cordes Brown examined and studied the blueprints of the world's deluxe hotels before he developed his "palace."

A prominent Denver architect, Frank E. Edbrooke, designed a building in the spirit of the Italian Renaissance. Because of the geometric pattern of Brown's land, the hotel took on an unusual shape. Edbrooke gave the building a tri-frontage and then planned it so that each room faced a street. Without any interior rooms, every guest could have a view, plus morning or afternoon sunshine! The contractors, Geddes and Serrie, constructed this soon-to-be famous landmark from Colorado red granite and

Brown Palace Hotel

warm brown Arizona sandstone. James Whitehouse then carved a lovely series of medallions in the stone.

Completed in 1892, the 10-story building had 400 rooms. Fireplaces were standard for each room, as well as bathroom taps yielding artesian water straight from the hotel's wells (as they still do today). The finest achievements in steam heating and electricity were incorporated into the structure. The Brown was also noted as the second fireproof edifice in the country.

It took four years and $1 million to complete Henry Brown's luxurious dream. Cool water flowed from the taps; steam heat provided warmth. Ice machines kept the wine chilled and the produce fresh. Turkish baths, hairdressing parlors, billiard rooms—even a hotel library!—were available for guest use. Linens, china, glassware, and silver came from the finest craftsmen. Carpets and curtains in each room had special designs. Excellence abounded at every turn.

The Brown Palace opened for a banquet of the Triennial Conclave of Knights Templar and their ladies. A seven-course dinner at $10 a plate was served in the main dining room on the eighth floor. The guests viewed more than 300 miles of Rocky Mountain grandeur from the wide dining-room windows.

Denver society was formally introduced to the Brown Palace a few months later when the Tabors threw a fancy ball. In the years since, the Brown has hosted thousands of such glittering evenings.

Today the Brown Palace Hotel is listed in the National Register of Historic Places. Even in the midst of modern times, it continues to provide guests with historical authenticity, Victorian charm, and good service. The original decor has been preserved, especially in the restaurants—the hallmarks of the hotel.

Conveniently located at Seventeenth and Tremont, the Brown Palace Hotel is in the heart of downtown Denver's financial and shopping district. Many sights and cultural points of interest are within walking distance. It pays to make reservations several weeks in advance. 321 Seventeenth Street, Denver 80202; (303) 297–3111 or (800) 321–2599.

The ◆ **Queen Anne Inn** is a favorite with honeymooners; *Modern Bride, Bride's,* and *Bridal Guide* sing its praises. Because this bed-and-breakfast is so close to Denver's financial district, bigtime quiet-seeking executives also stay here. The ten-room mansion has fetched accolades from bona fide historians.

And small wonder.

·This Victorian masterpiece dates back to 1879. Each of the bed chambers is different, yet all are crammed with genuine Victoriana: brass beds, canopied beds, four-poster beds, love seats, armoires, stained-glass windows, walnut tables, oak rocking chairs, and the like. (A touch of kitsch is occasionally sighted, too.)

The bed-and-breakfast ambience is carefully enhanced: a glass of fine sherry upon arrival, against a backdrop of piped-in chamber music; continental breakfast served (upon request) in bed on a white wicker tray, or breakfast with other travelers at the inn, or, weather permitting, in the garden.

The location of the three-storied mansion in the Clements Historic District couldn't be better. And for honeymooners, or the real tourists, there awaits a horse-and-buggy ride. For more information about the (expensive) accommodations, contact Queen Anne Inn, 2147 Tremont Place, Denver 80205; (303) 296–6666.

How would you like to have breakfast, enjoy Sunday brunch or weekday lunch or presupper snack or best of all—dinner!—in a Tudor-style castle overlooking the city of Denver and a green golf course? All this has been possible for almost two decades at the ♦ **Wellshire Inn.** And you can thank a restaurateur named Leo Goto for the locale and the eating pleasures. Goto transformed a run-down clubhouse into the tasteful English chateau with its heavy wooden doors; antique, colored leaded-glass windows; sparkling chandeliers; luxurious carpets; and dramatic fireplaces. The place radiates intimacy and true elegance. Baronial splendor! Four million dollars' worth of remodeling!

Several local critics have called the Wellshire Inn "one of Denver's most beautiful restaurants."

The decor is enhanced by the freshest available foods—romaine lettuce, spinach, Chinese vegetables, fruit, Mediterranean greens; the entrees—Tournedos Windsor, fresh salmon fillets, Italian-style Scampi, Chicken Dijon, Wellshire Chateaubriand, and Leo's famous Rack of Lamb—can only be called memorable. Scenic, pastoral views, country club atmosphere, good food, friendly service—can anyone ask for more?

Wellshire Inn, 3333 South Colorado Boulevard, Denver 80222; (303) 759–3333.

Washington Park—my favorite—on a late September morning. One of Colorado's poet laureates, at age ninety, was known to walk around one of the lakes here. Actually, it has started to snow. Winter without the benefit of fall. Yesterday the sun still blazed here, and now the flakes tumble thickly. The lake steams.

Normally filled with cyclists, the park is deserted. Denver's miniblizzard air is being washed clean by the moisture. A few hardy joggers, wool caps over their ears, jog along the lake paths. The grass is still too warm for the snow to stick; the wet meadows seem greener than at any other time of the year.

The miniblizzard stops. Clouds drift overhead.

Through the park you can see some of Denver's old homes of Downing, Louisiana, and Franklin streets. Typically, all the

141

houses come with lawns and gardens. The latter form the visitor's first impressions.

A weekday may be the best day to stroll through Denver's ◆**Washington Park,** at South Downing and East Virginia streets, not far from East Alameda Avenue. The wide expanse of green is almost unknown to tourists, despite all the delights here: Small creeks are shaded by willows and cottonwoods. Anything and everything happens at Washington Park on weekends: Young lovers from nearby Denver University walk along the paths; elderly gentlemen play a game of bocce in slow motion on a special well-kept lawn; young champions slam tennis balls across one of the many free courts; an entire family feeds ducks and geese. Washington Park has several playgrounds for small-fry, and plenty of picnic tables. Washington Park comes with ample flower beds that remind you of English gardens.

The park also boasts a large recreation center where you can swim indoors, work out in a gym with sophisticated machinery, join a basketball game, or, if you stay in town long enough, take various classes that range from puppetry to pottery. The modernistic recreation center is ideal for rainy days.

Happiness for Denverites is ◆**Sloan's Lake,** located between Sheridan Boulevard and Newton. The lakeshore and the grass fetch an elderly clientele—pensioners, retired railroad people, old Indians, some fishing out of their automobiles, others sitting near the water—as well as young Vietnamese.

No crowds during the week. Then on summer Saturdays a crescendo of people. The climax comes on July Sundays or holidays. From the Fourth of July to Labor Day, the parking lots cannot hold all the automobiles with picnickers and their baskets, with more anglers hoping for a ten-pound carp; teenagers ready to toss footballs, baseballs, plastic platters; ladies with grandchildren; three-year-olds waving bags of bread. Orange-beaked ducks waddle eagerly ashore; wild Canada geese float with nonchalance toward the toss of popcorn.

You see father-and-son teams playing—surprise!—a game of croquet; you see water-skiers in black wet suits. Windy days produce sailboats—thirty of them—fifty?—a regatta! Sailors ply the blue Sloan's Lake surface in their dinghies, Snipes, or Sunfish vessels. The joggers are always in evidence, too, and in any weather a few old, sometimes overweight couples walk around the lake—doctor's orders. On sunny days the Rockies wink in the background.

You can enter the park from West Seventeenth Avenue or from Sheridan Boulevard and from several other points, all west of Federal Boulevard and south of West Colfax Avenue.

Actually, Denver's municipal parks stimulate plenty of outdoor life on 2,800 acres; to these you may add another city-owned 14,000 acres in the foothills. Wildflowers! Spruce trees! Pines! Meadows!

Small wonder that Denver is called "The City of Green."

THE GREAT PLAINS

"Colorado? Ah, high peaks! Mountain towns! Skiing!" This is how many easterners, southerners, and midwesterners describe their idea of a state that has mountains on its license plates. Even Europeans know about the Rockies. The plains—especially Colorado's eastern plains, the farmer's domain—come as a surprise.

Yet much of the land belongs to agriculture. As you drive east from Denver, Colorado Springs, Pueblo, Trinidad, the country takes on the flat character of Kansas and Nebraska, with which Colorado shares its eastern border. The names turn rural: Punkin Center, Wild Horse, Deer Trail.

Communities like Wray, Holyoke, and Yuma all got their start through homesteading. About 94 percent of Colorado's land consists of dry or irrigated farmlands, rangeland, and forests.

Eastern Colorado was first settled during the middle and late 1880s. Little agricultural communities like Haxtun, Kiowa, and Eads sprang up. Oats, barley, wheat, and corn were planted; harvesting was done with primitive machinery. Some of the farms were the result of the early railroads selling cheap tracts of land to immigrants.

The homesteaders fought hard financial battles when the droughts hit in 1890. But the Homestead Act, which presented volunteer farmers with 160 free acres, was a big incentive in Colorado. Many of the settlers demanded few luxuries from their homesteads. They tilled, planted, harvested, and faced blizzards and hailstorms, grasshoppers and more droughts. The worst ones hit during the 1920s.

Still, through the years, eastern Colorado produced not just corn and wheat but also dry beans, alfalfa, potatoes, onions, rye, sorghum, and commercial vegetables. In Rocky Ford, year after year, the citizens grew watermelons and cantaloupes.

The farmers endured the summer heat and dust storms. World War II was good to the Colorado farm economy. New well-drilling techniques and irrigation improved the situation. During the 1960s wheat sales hit record figures. The 1970s brought prosperity. The export trade flourished. Land prices soared. Farmers splurged on newfangled $100,000 machinery.

When exports shrunk, as everywhere in the Midwest and West, the Colorado farmers suffered. The 1980s were harsh to the eastern part of the state. Prices dropped for crops, while everything else cost more.

Yet some farmers survived. A few lucky ones—close to cities like Denver, Fort Morgan, and Sterling—switched to sod farming.

They create instant lawns for suburbia, as an adjunct to the housing explosion. Near Parker you see miles and miles of green carpets, well watered, neatly rolled up, ready for shipment. New homes still go up in Englewood, Littleton, Aurora, Thornton, and Castle Rock, and each new house clamors for its swath of green, often supplied by sod farmers.

Others stay on and grow "Hard Red" winter wheat and specialty items like asparagus, flowers, peas, and sunflower seeds. A small number build greenhouses or mushroom cellars. Dry beans and millet bring profits.

Others sell out to giants, go bankrupt, or seek jobs in the city. Third-generation farmers sometimes give up; regretfully, their children move to town. Some are lucky enough to sell their land to developers of condos and shopping centers. One well-known dairy farmer plans to develop the land himself. Farmers turn into land managers for absentee agribusiness owners. The Colorado farm wives, meanwhile, try to hold the marriages together. If they're lucky, they can still see their men out there, in the field under the open sky, working from dawn to dusk.

The scenery packs little excitement. Abandoned houses, an occasional silo, and fields in all directions. Grain elevator. Weighing station. Plows holding court. Small communities where one automatically slows down for the sights of feed stores or an old twelve-unit motel or the cafe with home cooking.

Many of the little hamlets in eastern Colorado seem alike. Small houses with porches. Shop windows with tools, placed there helter-skelter. After nine at night almost everything is closed. Main Street is so silent that you can hear the crickets in the field.

Each little town has several churches, which get busy on Sunday. Sermons on your car radio. A quick glance through a picture window shows a farmer watching a television evangelist. Does the preacher have an answer when the banks want their money? Or when the man's farm is to be auctioned off to his creditors next week?

The inhabitants of eastern Colorado are reserved, not too friendly, perhaps distrustful, certainly preoccupied. But they have time. "Oh, sure," says one of them to an inquirer from the city. "Sure, we have problems. But there's more space to have them in."

Most visitors—and even new immigrants to Colorado—think the state consists mostly of Denver and suburbs and perhaps a few mountain towns like Vail and Aspen. They often forget northern and eastern Colorado. When Mark Twain visited in 1862, however, he reveled in the prairie and the horses. "It was a noble sport galloping over the plain in the dewy freshness of the morning," Twain wrote.

The dewy freshness is still there, along with the star-filled sky, some farms with their tilled fields, the big cottonwoods. Despite the giant interstate highways, the air is still pure. Unlike in Denver, where the car-caused pollution backs up against the mountains, the breezes from the northwest do a fine purification job. The cities of Fort Collins, Greeley, and Longmont have expanded; luckily, however, there is very little smokestack industry. You see new shopping malls and Holiday Inns and Kentucky Fried Chicken outposts. The tourists flock to communities such as Loveland, with its lakes and access to Rocky Mountain National Park.

In the same region, Fort Collins may well be the most sophisticated community in northern Colorado. With 87,800 inhabitants, it is the largest. Hordes of eager, serious Colorado State University students are here, and the visitor quickly becomes aware of wider interests: Fort Collins has several bookstores, numerous foreign-car dealers, and shops catering to the young. The distance to Denver is a manageable 66 miles.

Much of Colorado's famous corn-fed beef comes from Fort Collins. The dry climate is ideal for the Hereford and Angus cattle, and northern Colorado cattle feeders have worked out precise feeding systems. From this region the aged beef is shipped all over the world.

In recent years the area's ranchers have adapted themselves to the times. They now raise calves that are leaner and less cholesterol-laden. Low-fat feeding methods are in. Marbled meat is out. Moreover, some of these contemporary cattlemen shun growth stimulants and avoid antibiotics.

The Fort Collins–based Colorado State University is strong on agriculture and also trains forestry students, whose tree nurseries one can visit. The city has its own symphony orchestra and a theater. "We're often underestimated," says one Fort Collins official. "We shouldn't be. We're a microcosm of Denver, but without the air pollution and crime."

Just south is ◆ **Loveland,** only half the size of Fort Collins, yet it has carved a national name for itself. Loveland calls itself "Colorado's Sweetheart City."

Each year many sacks of valentines are being remailed here; the sentimental souls who send these love messages are backed by the town's civic leaders, who volunteer their time. Tradition! Cupid has worked here for some four decades. Loveland's postmasters themselves often create the corny poems that appear in cachet form next to the Loveland stamp. A typical verse:

> *The day is full of gladness*
> *And eyes with stardust shine*
> *When Cupid works his magic*
> *In this lovely valentine.*

The Loveland Post Office patiently copes with the extra work of some 400,000 valentines with the blessing of the town officials. Local high schools paint heart signs. On the Chamber of Commerce maps, Loveland appears in the shape of a heart, and the yearly "Miss Valentine" wears hearts on her apron. The local business community has no objections; there are now even Sweetheart shops and a Sweetheart Lane. Ironically, Loveland was named after a railroad robber baron.

Actually, agriculture and tourism go on strongly here, too: you spot cornfields and sugar beets, ride horses at local stables, use local campgrounds, and visit the numerous Loveland recreation areas. And the thousands of valentines via "Cupid's Hometown" or "The Valentine Capital of the World" are a business by themselves.

146

The city of Greeley (founded by Horace Greeley, the newspaper publisher) is a few miles to the east of Loveland. Greeley was meant to become an agricultural colony, too, and succeeded. All around the town's perimeter, you see sugar-beet fields, barley, and other crops.

Much of the local sightseeing harks back to agriculture. At the (summer-only) ◆**Centennial Village,** the curators erected a sod house, a homesteader's wagon house, and a one-room rural school. The Greeley Public library displays photos of assorted ethnic immigrant farm families. Rodeos are popular, and Greeley's annual Weld Fair has livestock shows complete with poultry, rabbits, sheep, and displays of various field crops.

To be sure, James Michener was inspired to write his bestselling novel *Centennial* through his familiarity and on-location research in Greeley and surroundings.

Michener's fictional pioneers built their town of Centennial on the Platte River. The story is one of struggle, success, failure, and, above all, endurance. Perhaps the closest thing to his invented Centennial is the near–ghost town of Keota, Colorado, 40 miles northeast of Greeley. Michener returned to Keota more than a dozen times to absorb its atmosphere and talk with postmaster Clyde Stanley.

Stanley had lived in Keota most of his seventy years. He had seen the eager farmers come, only to be displaced by drought and dust storms. He watched the town dwindle from 129 people in 1929 to 6 in 1970. Michener dedicated the book to Stanley, "who introduced me to the prairie."

Not many people—or even Michener's readers—realize that the famous author had good reasons to turn to Greeley and northwestern Colorado for his research. In 1936, at the age of twenty-nine and not yet a writer, Michener taught in Greeley at what was to become the University of Northern Colorado.

He never regretted his decision. "In Greeley, I grew up spiritually, emotionally, intellectually," he later noted in John P. Hayes's *James A. Michener: A Biography.*

While there, Michener became friends with Floyd Merrill, Greeley's newspaper editor. The pair made almost weekly ventures into the surrounding country. At least three times a month, Merrill and the future bestselling author took off for exploration to the intricate irrigation systems that produced Colorado's vegetables and fruit, sometimes to the mountains. "We would look down into valleys crowded with blue spruce and aspen, and quite often out onto the prairie east of town where majestic buttes rose starkly from the barren waste," Michener relates in Hayes's biography.

Merrill also taught the young professor to use a camera. Michener credits the photos he took in Colorado with keeping his images of the West alive and vital long enough for *Centennial* to be conceived.

Already well known in 1970, the author returned to Colorado, determined to write an exhaustive story of the western experience. He explored the natural and social history of the region.

And he made northeastern Colorado famous.

One of the landmarks in his book *Centennial* is the fictitious "Rattlesnake Buttes." "They were extraordinary, these two sentinels of the plains. Visible for miles in each direction, they guarded a bleak and sad empire," Michener wrote.

These promontories exist and are known as the ◆ **Pawnee Buttes,** part of the Pawnee National Grassland. Administered by the Forest Service, the grasslands encompasses more then 200,000 acres.

The wind here is nearly constant. The terrain made history in the 1930s when drifts of wind-driven topspoil piled up like snow over fences, closing roads and killing crops.

This Pawnee grassland was born from tragedy.

A gravel road takes you to the "Buttes" trailhead. From there a 1½-mile path takes you on foot or by mountain bike to the first butte, the western one. The eastern butte lies ¼ mile east. From a plateau the trail drops to the prairie floor, crossing open pastureland, then dropping again into a deep ravine. Cream-colored chalk cliffs form the promontories. Call it a short-grass prairie here, somewhat like a tundra. The steadily moving air masses keep growths low to the ground. Prickly pear cactus, blue gramma grass, sagebrush, and buffalo grass grow no higher then 6 inches.

Lack of water and trees do not prevent many species of birds from flourishing in this country. Lark buntings—the Colorado State bird, with its distinctive white wing patches against a black body—thrive here. So do horned larks, meadowlarks, kestrels, mountain plovers, common nighthawks, and long-billed curlews—some of the 200 species recorded here. A 36-mile self-guided birding tour is a great ride over the prairie in a high-clearance car or on a mountain bike. Cattle share this area with pronghorn antelope and windmill-powered water tanks for stock. For information contact the District Ranger, Pawnee National Grassland, 660 O Street, Suite A, Greeley 80631; (303) 353–5004.

The eastern plains of Colorado saw some of the most travel activity and bloodshed occurring in the early days of this country. Indians, trappers, traders, settlers, Mexicans, and the Spanish used what was called the Santa Fe Trail, which followed along the Arkansas River for many miles.

The Bent, St. Vrain and Company, a frontier trading and retailing business, built and owned ◆**Bent's Old Fort** near what is now La Junta. The fort was a trading place for Mexicans, Indians, and trappers. Mexico got quality manufactured goods from the United States. The Indians got cookware, metal, rifles, and other goods. Trappers obtained supplies, a market for their furs, and the company of other people following lonely months of hunting. The Bent, St. Vrain and Company traded with all these people and they among themselves. Furs and buffalo robes were sold back east.

In the mid-1800s, Bent's Old Fort was caught between resentful Indians and the white people who were moving in on them. The Indian wars began and the trade faded away. Charles Bent was killed in a revolt in Taos, New Mexico. St. Vrain left to do business further south. Cholera spread through the Indian tribes. William Bent, the remaining partner, left, a disillusioned and disappointed man. Bent's Old Fort fell into ruins.

Designated by the National Park Service as a National Historic Site, Bent's Old Fort has been rebuilt almost exactly as it had been constructed originally. Authentic materials and tools were used in the reconstruction. Today the adobe structure remains a monument to past and present-day craftspeople whose skill and patience built and rebuilt it again.

Just outside La Junta, Bent's Old Fort stands as it did almost one hundred years ago. To preserve the authentic atmosphere of this trade center, visitor parking is ¼ mile from the building. The long paved walk toward the fort, with its backdrop of cottonwood trees by the Arkansas River, takes you into history.

In deference to realism there are no concessions for food, drink, or curios. In fact, you begin to believe the only bathroom may be the one reconstructed as part of the fort. But not to worry. Tucked into a corner are modern toilets and water fountains. A small bookstore exhibits numerous historical volumes.

The building is truly a fort. Four high walls surround a central courtyard. Entrance is through an archway with huge wooden doors. The two levels in the fort contain mostly community rooms, including the well room, trade room, dining area and kitchen, wash house, warehouses, and blacksmith's and laborer's tiny quarters. Other quarters are on the second level, providing more privacy and ventilation. Corrals at the back held military horses and some cattle.

Uniformed park employees are on hand to answer questions. But to get into the spirit of the place, join one of the free guided tours conducted by an individual dressed in period clothes. These "interpreters" stay in character, thanks to the authentic costumes. Their tour will be informative and will make you feel like you lived here in the 1880s. Small fee. Scheduled special events go on all year, such as the "Fur Trade Encampment," a mountain-man type of rendezvous in July.

For more information: Bent's Old Fort, National Historic Site, 35110 Highway 194 East, La Junta 81050-9523; (719) 384–2596.

For a trip even further back into history—150 million years further back—visit the longest set of dinosaur tracks known in the world. About 25 miles south of La Junta is ◆ **Picketwire Canyon** in Comanche National Grasslands. Picketwire opened to the public in 1991. The attraction? The clear footprints of dinosaurs on a solidified limestone shelf just a few feet over the Purgatory River.

Guided motorized tours are available. They are free, but you must provide your own four-wheel-drive vehicle. Also space is extremely limited. Most openings are filled a year in advance. Otherwise, no motorized access has been allowed in this highly restricted area. It's limited because of concern about preserving the footprints.

If you don't have a four-wheel-drive vehicle or can't get on one of the tours, there is another possibility, a bit more strenuous but worth the effort. Mountain biking and hiking are allowed in Picketwire. From a parking area near a cattle pen, an 8-mile ranch road takes the biker/hiker across a high mesa, then drops suddenly into the canyon. As you follow along, the relics of abandoned adobe houses, a church, a graveyard, and ranch buildings hold up against the dry climate.

This area get very hot in the summer, and rattlesnakes are a real hazard. This is, however, an ideal trip on a mountain bike. Would-be hikers should consider this almost 17-mile round-trip. Long! Using a bike you can zip along the dusty road and catch glimpses of the current inhabitants: a coyote, kestrels, orioles. I never saw a snake, but I also didn't go into the tall grass where they nap. The dinosaur tracks are marked by small signs pointing the way. Right next to the river, you come to a shelf of limestone that looks like someone mucked around in it while it was wet. On further examination you discover that these muddlings are dinosaur tracks. You may have to clean the dirt and sand out to truly determine that these are dinosaur tracks. The brontosaurus left big holes like you'd expect from an elephant, yet much bigger. The meat-eating allosaurus left distinctive three-toed, wicked-looking footprints.

It's hot in this Colorado country. Take plenty of water and a hat to put on after you take off your bike helmet. Expect to spend about three hours for the round-trip. But also expect to be alone. The guided tours don't use the bike route. There are no human inhabitants of this area now. Overnight camping is verboten.

Petroglyphs dot the rock canyon walls. These rock etchings aren't identified by signs; you just have to find them on your own. If time is important, do this trip for the dinosaur tracks. Try to walk in their footprints, left more than 150 million years ago. Contact the U.S. Forest Service, Comanche National Grassland, P.O. Box 817, La Junta 81050; (719) 384–2181.

INDEX

ACKNOWLEDGMENTS

This book was written with the help of many people. The author would like to thank Richard Grant, Denver Metro Convention and Visitors Bureau; Bill Saul, National Western Stock Show; Kathryn Toomey, Golden researcher; Roi Davis, Buckhorn Exchange and Museum; Leo Goto, Wellshire Inn; Lillian Wyles, Denver researcher; JoAnn Sims, Central City Opera House Association; Elena Valdez, Aspen Ritz Carlton Hotel; Killeen Russell, Aspen Public Affairs; J. S. Munn, Vista Verde; Bill Sageser, Tamarron; Christy Metz, National Park Service; Dave Smith, Hi Country Haus Resort; Kristine Meyer, Beaver Village and Preferred Properties, Winter Park; Susan Stiff, Westin Hotels in Vail and Denver; Robert Levine, and Bert Farin, Antlers Lionshead; Ray Schafer, Manor Vail; Paula Sheridan, Winter Park Resort; Kristine L. Bittner, researcher and editorial assistant; and finally, Helen Evans, my special travel companion.

About the Author

A Denver resident, Curtis Casewit has written more than forty books, eight of them travel guides. He writes travel columns regularly for newspapers nationwide and lectures at several writing workshops during the summer. He taught creative writing at the University of Colorado for thirty years.

UNITED STATES TRAVEL
Off the Beaten Path™ Series

These are the fine guides from our
Off the Beaten Path™ series designed for the traveler who
enjoys the special and unusual. Each book is by an author
who knows the state well, did extensive research, and personally visited many of the places, often more than once.
Please check your local bookstore for fine
Globe Pequot Press titles, which include:

Alabama, $9.95	Missouri, $9.95
Arkansas, $9.95	Montana, $9.95
Colorado, $9.95	New Hampshire, $9.95
Connecticut, $9.95	New Jersey, $9.95
Florida, $9.95	New Mexico, $9.95
Georgia, $9.95	New York, $8.95
Hawaii, $10.95	North Carolina, $9.95
Illinois, $9.95	Northern California, $9.95
Indiana, $9.95	Ohio, $9.95
Iowa, $9.95	Oregon, $9.95
Kansas, $9.95	Pennsylvania, $9.95
Kentucky, $9.95	Southern California, $8.95
Louisiana, $9.95	Tennessee, $9.95
Maine, $9.95	Vermont, $9.95
Maryland, $9.95	Virginia, $9.95
Massachusetts, $9.95	Washington, $9.95
Michigan, $9.95	Wisconsin, $9.95
Minnesota, $9.95	

To order any of these titles with MASTERCARD or VISA,
call toll-free (800) 243–0495; in Connecticut call (800)
962–0973. Free shipping for orders of three or more books.
Shipping charge of $3.00 per book for one or two books
ordered. Connecticut residents add sales tax. Ask for your
free catalogue of Globe Pequot's quality books on recreation, travel, nature, gardening, cooking, crafts, and more.
Prices and availability subject to change.